PENGUIN

AUSTRALIAN SUMMER STORIES 3

PENGUIN
AUSTRALIAN SUMMER STORIES 3

PENGUIN BOOKS

Penguin Books Australia Ltd
487 Maroondah Highway, PO Box 257
Ringwood, Victoria 3134, Australia
Penguin Books Ltd
Harmondsworth, Middlesex, England
Penguin Putnam Inc.
375 Hudson Street, New York, New York 10014, USA
Penguin Books Canada Limited
10 Alcorn Avenue, Toronto, Ontario, Canada M4V 3B2
Penguin Books (NZ) Ltd
Cnr Rosedale and Airborne Roads, Albany, Auckland, New Zealand
Penguin Books (South Africa) (Pty) Ltd
5 Watkins Street, Denver Ext. 4, 2094, South Africa
Penguin Books India (P) Ltd
11, Community Centre, Panchsheel Park, New Delhi 100 017, India

First published by Penguin Books Australia Ltd 2000

10 9 8 7 6 5 4 3 2 1

Copyright in this collection © Penguin Books Australia Ltd 2001
Copyright in individual stories remains with the authors

The moral right of the authors has been asserted.

All rights reserved. Without limiting the rights under copyright reserved above, no part of this publication may be reproduced, stored in or introduced into a retrieval system, or transmitted, in any form or by any means (electronic, mechanical, photocopying, recording or otherwise), without the prior written permission of both the copyright owner and the above publisher of this book.

Cover design by Jenny Grigg, Penguin Design Studio
Typeset in Sabon by Midland Typesetters, Maryborough, Victoria
Printed and bound in Australia by Australian Print Group, Maryborough, Victoria

National Library of Australia
Cataloguing-in-Publication data:

Penguin Australian summer stories. 3.

ISBN 0 14 100258 1.

1. Summer – Fiction. 2. Short stories, Australian. I. Title: Australian Summer Stories.

A823.010833

This project has been assisted by the Commonwealth Government through the Australia Council, its arts funding and advisory body.

www.penguin.com.au

CONTENTS

LIFE WITH SEA VIEWS Michelle de Kretser	1
DINGLE THE FOOL Elizabeth Jolley	14
INCIDENT IN THE HOTEL TANGIER Matt Condon	32
MERMAID BEACH Julie Simpson	40
THE ABSOLUTE AUTHORITY ON EVERYTHING Derek Hansen	44
THEATRE COMES TO WOMBAT CREEK Amy Witting	72

VILLA ADRIANA Shirley Hazzard	87
EILEEN'S CHRISTMAS FUDGE Gillian Mears	96
TEA AND BISCUITS WITH RICHIE BENAUD Chris Daffey	105
THE WASTELAND Frank Dalby Davison	119
THE HAIRCUT OF A MORE SUCCESSFUL MAN Nick Earls	135
FIVE UNUSUAL JOURNEYS Elizabeth Stead	148
CLOSER David Malouf	159
ALL THOSE BLOODY YOUNG CATHOLICS Helen Garner	169
PIPE DREAM Chandani Lokugé	176

WHAT ARE THE ROOTS THAT CLUTCH   185
Matthew Karpin

A TASTE FOR IT   197
Monica McInerney

THE KISS   211
Peter Goldsworthy

NOTES ON THE CONTRIBUTORS   232

ACKNOWLEDGEMENTS   237

LIFE WITH SEA VIEWS

MICHELLE DE KRETSER

They lived in a brown house on a green hill. At twilight bats swooped through lighted rooms and the little girls shrieked and covered their heads with their arms.

Beyond the fields lay the railway line, curving along the coast. While they slept under mosquito nets, cotton nighties tangled about their thighs, the night mail whistled round the bend. Limbs in flight, they dreamt of journeys (the promise of leaving, the sadness of arrival).

*

The tennis court was next to the railway station, separated from it by a grey-gone-green wall. Girls in white uniforms and pipeclayed tennis shoes ran about, hitting out with heavy wooden racquets. From time to time, they came to a halt: 'Our ball, please? Could we have our ball, please?' And someone, waiting for a train, would throw it back to their voices.

Halfway through a set, Monique looked up and saw that the sky had turned indigo. The sun still blazed overhead, an orange disc, slightly flattened and translucent like a sweet sucked thin.

Beyond the railway line was the sea. You couldn't see it, but you knew it was there: salt, secret, waiting for you like time.

★

Ned arrived late, after his parents had given up hope. He was a beautiful child, all dimples and lashes. Unable to do otherwise, the girls adored him. But sometimes Estelle seethed, whispering 'You are the fruit of withered loins' in her brother's ear. Then, overcome, she would kiss him until he grew bored and tugged away.

★

They never played under the palm trees because there was a little girl who did and a coconut fell on her head and her brains came out through her nose.

★

Monique learnt the cello, piano and violin. She liked the violin best, because it was her father's instrument. He had belonged to the municipal orchestra until a new conductor arrived and asked him to resign. As the only left-handed musician, he was spoiling the symmetrical bowing of the string section.

Estelle excelled at Speech & Drama. Her *Quality of Mercy* took first prize in the inter-school competition and her picture appeared in the local paper. She had a small mole near the corner of one eye, like a tear. Her favorite color was crimson, which is not suitable for a young girl.

*

The electricity faltered and failed. While they waited for candles, Ned plunged his hands into the ice-box and then, coming noiselessly up behind Estelle, closed cold fingers around her throat. It was a long time before she would speak to him again.

*

Rosemarie S. was Captain of Games and had ropy, light-brown hair. Monique suddenly realised she could not do without Rosie, trailing her around at recess with a small group of the similarly afflicted.

She climbed the hill, books tied with a buckled strap and balanced in the crook of her arm. She had stayed late, for hockey practice. Rounding the bend, she came upon Father pitched head-first into a clump of oleanders. The soles of his shoes had worn thin on the instep, where his weight rolled over when he walked. Just like Ned's.

Rosie gave Monique her hanky, chain-stitched with a blue R. Ripples spread through the lower forms and Claudine G. said loudly that everyone had known about that black woman from the fishing shanties.

*

Money had to be set aside for Ned's education, there was never any question about that. But they had to let three servants go.

*

The girls stood side by side on the beach with their skirts tucked up, and waves sucked at the sand beneath their bare feet. They swayed deliciously on the curved rim of the world.

*

The magistrate's daughter fell into the road when the rickshaw puller stumbled in a pothole. She landed on her head, but picked herself up, climbed back in and continued on her way. That evening she complained of a headache and asked for an Aspro. Then she lay down on the cement floor and died. The rickshaw puller got nine years.

The gardener's wife jumped down a well. That was the usual way among women of that type. Handy, cost nothing, didn't involve blood.

Ned, walking barefoot on the lawn as he was not supposed to do because of hookworm, felt a squishiness beneath his toes. He had trodden on a chameleon lying there on the grass with its inside outside.

*

Gordon L. smiled at Monique during choir practice. They were both invited to a party, with dancing on the lantern-hung veranda and frangipani scenting the night. When he called at the house, he sat on the left-hand side of the sofa. Monique sat on the right-hand side and Monique's mother sat between them.

Shortly afterwards Gordon L. qualified as a civil engineer, married a girl with buck teeth and took up a post in the interior.

*

Sundays as interminable as the view from the veranda.

*

The cost of living was what came of ignorant villagers voting for people who didn't even wear suits.

*

Monique's certificates from Trinity College, London, hung

above the piano, next to the photograph of the Queen. After school and all day on Saturdays children came and went from the house, dropped off by chauffeurs or toiling up the hill with violin cases and music under their arms.

Estelle said that she hoped whoever wrote *Für Elise* was still answering for it.

*

Ned was sent to board with relatives. Everyone stood weeping on the platform. But the decent schools were in the capital, ninety-nine miles away.

Ned couldn't eat a hardboiled egg if shelling had left even the tiniest imperfection on its surface. Nor would he accept marrow that had been cooked, extracted from the bone and spread glistening on toast. There were many such difficulties, relayed by his aunt in tight-lipped letters.

*

The monsoon brought a cyclone that lashed the south. Tiles were blown off the roof, and rain overflowed from basins placed hazardously throughout the house. The shantytown flooded. A tidal wave was feared. They sat on the veranda looking out over the swollen grey expanse of sky and sea, straining to make out the invisible horizon. What would they do if it reared up to embrace their hill? Where can you hide from so much water?

*

There was a Grow More Food campaign. Buses carried Ned's year to paddy fields where they stood ankle-deep in muddy water, splashing each other and pulling out the weeds that sprouted between the tender shoots of rice. A government official rushed around trying to minimise the damage. Finally he retreated to the shade. Encouraging the urban young to appreciate farming was one thing, but in his opinion the farmers weren't enjoying it much.

*

The nuns ran a hostel in the capital. When Estelle left there was a floating sensation in Monique's chest. As if her heart had worked loose from its moorings, was riding anchorless on the tide.

*

His aunt detected 'cheap liquor' on Ned's breath.

*

So many rooms that no one entered.

*

Monique, at the station to farewell friends, saw a tall, good-looking stranger leap on to the platform before the train had quite come to a halt. He advanced on her party with a smile, running his hand through his curls: why, it was Ned.

She was troubled by a dream in which she hurried after her father down unfamiliar streets hemmed in by huddled houses. But when he turned around she saw a man with coarse dark features, whose thick-wristed hands shot out towards her.

*

Everyone who could leave was going.

Islands are the places you set out from. Continents are where you arrive.

*

Estelle came home for Christmas wearing an electric-blue pantsuit. 'Come back with me,' she pleaded. 'Three months to get your shorthand-typing certificate and then you'll be set.'

Their mother wouldn't leave her room, not even when Ned wanted to carry her out on to the veranda for the fireworks. She pressed her hand to her pintucked bosom and murmured that it would only be a matter of time. They sat around her bed, listening to distant explosions.

'There's a band every night at the Coconut Grove,' said Estelle, 'there are cocktails and foreigners.' 'I'm not staying,' said Estelle dabbing perfume behind her ears, 'and you wouldn't either, if you had any sense.'

*

Ned failed his varsity entrance for the third time. It was decided he would apply to the railways. The problem with the railways, as everyone knew, was drink. On the other hand, there was the pension.

*

She learnt to sleep lightly. Her mother often rapped on the wall, wanting a different arrangement of pillows or to be helped to the bathroom.

Afterwards, Monique would go out on to the veranda. Gradually, the sea detached itself from the coast, a different blackness. Sometimes there were ships, their lights like coded messages far out towards the horizon.

*

Estelle's engagement ring was an opal because of Harry being Australian.

*

There were young foreigners everywhere, with too much dirty hair and shapeless clothes. One of them tipped a boy from the shanties a hundred for running an errand. Some fellow from the market set up four bamboo poles on the beach, slung palm thatching over them and called it a restaurant. Next thing he was making money hand over fist. That class of person has no shame.

Now at night there was a string of colored bulbs on the beach. Laughter. That music they liked drifting up the dark hill. Monique drew her housecoat close around her shoulders. People were right to call it disturbing.

★

Further down the coast was a palm tree with two heads. It was so tall that it was visible from the veranda, its twin heads like enormous feathery flowers swaying above the distant, uniform green.

That year lightning struck the tree one night, splitting its trunk and bringing it crashing on to the railway tracks. So that the next morning it was gone, the skyline jolted into difference.

★

There were few visitors now. The hill was daunting and so many people could no longer afford a car. The nuns still called, of course, hardship was no more than they expected; and Father André, roaring up on his dusty motorcycle.

★

A flimsy blue airletter came every fortnight if the Emergency hadn't disrupted the post. Estelle's writing was neat, spiky, illegible. It took a day or more to puzzle out a letter in its entirety. Even then, obscurities remained: 'lamingtons', 'nature strip'.

Ned turned up now and then. He would sit by his

mother's bed in the shuttered room, holding her hand and telling her about the places he had been to on the trains. He could always make her laugh, with his stories of jumped-up stationmasters and the explanations people offered for travelling without a ticket. He kept the bottle on the veranda and slipped out from time to time.

Once, after one of these visits, their mother asked Monique if she had noticed Ned's hands. It was the only time they ever mentioned it.

*

The shantytown was bulldozed one morning. The new hotel was rising slowly within its bamboo scaffolding and the shanties were an eyesore.

*

At the musical evening Corinne V. disgraced herself by breaking down halfway through her piece, that Chopin prelude in E minor. The child was hopeless, not a musical bone in her, she never practised and sat there slapping sulkily at mosquitoes when you tried to explain anything. No wonder she didn't get through the exam. But parents don't see it like that, of course, they blame the teacher.

How many pupils did that leave?

*

Estelle wrote that 'things hadn't worked out' with Harry. Hadn't worked out! But she had met someone called – could it be Sloven? – and promised to send a cheque as soon as she was 'back on her feet'.

*

Four headless bodies washed up on the beach. One of them was a woman; you could imagine what the soldiers had done before they'd finished with her. Not that you could blame them for cracking down after those suicide bombs in the city.

*

The ward had once been painted an insipid green. Hospital green, thought Ned, that was what his mother called that color. People lay on iron beds and also on straw mats on the floor in between. There was the smell of bedpans, and of the meals brought in for patients by their families. A pair of wasps building a nest high in one corner of the ceiling flew in and out through the barred window.

Damp and other things had drawn islands and continents on the green wall. If he tried he could make out the outline of a ship, the old kind with three masts. It reminded him that when he was a boy he had hung entranced over maps, dreaming of sailing to Australia. Funny how things you'd thought you'd forgotten were only stored away, waiting to swim into the light. Like opening a battered old chest with brass corners and coming on treasure kept safe, while the sea plucked and called in whispers.

There were dolphins on the wall and snakes as thick as a man's arm, with dragon heads. He pulled the coverlet closer. He was the boy on the bowsprit. They were sailing towards the horizon.

*

Claudine G. wheezed all the way up the hill in her too-tight red shoes to say that her cousin, over on holiday, had 'run into' Estelle. Monique hadn't mentioned that her sister was living in sin with a communist, had it slipped her mind? Apparently Estelle hadn't even been wearing mourning, although it had been only a few weeks after Ned.

All this while occupying the best chair, helping herself uninvited to another biscuit and drinking three cups of tea (four spoons of rationed sugar apiece).

*

'Father,' she called, weak with longing. But then he turned around.

*

Tourists stopped coming just when the hotel was completed. It stood vast and echoing, a ghost ship marooned on the reef of history. Slime spread up the sides of its empty swimming pools. Waves smashing against rocks sent spray arching through broken windows. The developer had hanged himself alongside the chandelier in the dining-room. No one went near the place after dark.

*

There were days when she woke to find that the sea had seeped in while she slept. Sea music washed through her, advancing, retreating, a rush followed by a swirl. She picked up her violin and tried to keep pace with it. The man selling snake beans was staring at her. She counted her change carefully, still humming.

*

In her good poplin dress, carrying an umbrella to protect her complexion, she picked her way down the main road. They kept her waiting thirty-seven minutes. The manager upended his plump little palms to signify apology and helplessness. What about the land, she asked, holding a chain-stitched handkerchief to her lips. He reminded her gently that it had already been sold.

The neighbors sent their sevant to say her sister would be ringing back in ten minutes. 'What is there to stay for now?' asked a voice that was nothing like Estelle's. 'We'll send your ticket,' said the voice, 'Stefan will fit out the bungalow for you.' The neighbors' children nudged each other and giggled in the doorway. Somewhere a woman was crying, saying if only they hadn't been away when the news about Mother.

*

The new flats had taken a lopsided slice out of the view. But at night you could still stand on the veranda and imagine the whole hill floating out to sea, houses, oleanders, telephone poles, its cargo of sleeping people rocking dreamily on the swell.

*

It was obvious from her clothes and the way she hovered on the edge of the veranda that she was a common village woman. She began explaining that she had done her best, but the man she was going to marry didn't know about the boy, and anyway it was only right for him to be with his own people.

He stood beside his mother, clinging to her hand. He was wearing navy-blue shorts and a clean white shirt, and clutched a brown-paper parcel. At length he lifted his head, and Ned's eyes peered up at Monique.

*

Father André was in violation of the dusk-to-dawn curfew, so the soldiers poured kerosene over him and set him alight.

*

Now in the dream she was on a complicated journey that took her through a series of smaller and smaller rooms until she stepped through a window and found him waiting for her, a wild sky and creeping water.

Waking, she slid her tongue over her lips and tasted salt.

*

The envelopes gathered in a brass tray on the hall table. When the rains came she opened some of the letters and folded them into paper boats. These she launched from the edge of the veranda into the overflow from the gutter, consigning them to light and change.

*

She had spoken to the boy once, to order him off the lawn. He was frightened of her smell and of the knotted purple veins on her skinny white legs. He kept to the back part of the house, where the cook slipped him slices of mango sprinkled with chilli.

He had not really been asleep when the noise woke him. At first he was afraid, because he had told himself in the daytime that the house must be haunted. But there was bright moonlight in the curtainless room, so after a while he crept to the window. He was just in time to see her go past, her violin under her chin, her left arm bowing.

Long after she had gone out of sight, he could hear the music wavering up the hill. Then the night mail came whistling round the bend.

DINGLE THE FOOL

ELIZABETH JOLLEY

'No one can tell what is taken up from the earth by a lemon tree.' Deirdre's mother said it didn't matter where the roots of the tree were, the lemons would take what they needed.

'What if they are in the drain?' Deirdre asked.

'What if they are?' her mother replied. 'Can you see drains on any of them lemons? Can you?'

Deirdre stood under the tree. It was fragrant with flower and fruit at the same time, she liked to be sent to fetch a lemon.

When Deirdre took off the cushion covers to wash them before Christmas, roses and peacocks from her childhood spilled out, frayed, from the worn covers underneath, reminding her of the tranquillity in that expectation of happiness as she and her sister Joanna, years ago, sat on the back veranda twisting tinsel and making red and green paper chains.

Now Deirdre remembered her mother most around Christmas. At that time of the year the sisters stole mulberries from the tree in the garden next to theirs and their mother, approving, made pies.

'Take Dingle to the river while I'm baking,' Mother called to them, so they took their brother out with them. They called him Dingle, it was his own name for himself. 'Dingle!' Mother called him softly, smiling at his gentle face. 'Always look after Dingle,' she told the girls. 'Remember, people will say he is a fool and will try to take away anything he's got. And he will give them everything.'

He loved the river. He shouted on the shore and waded into the brackish water, waving his thin arms and following the other children, he wanted to play with them. The other children swam and Dingle followed them, unable to swim. He waded deeper and the gentle waves slapped his knees and then caressed his waist and he held up his arms as he went deeper and then the water was round his neck and over his face and his round mouth gasped as the water closed and parted, rippling over his shorn head.

'Dingle! Deirdre shouted and ran into the river and grabbed him. She had to carry him home, her dress sopping wet, embarrassed because she was big and her breasts showed up round and heavy under the wet clinging material.

After the death of their mother the three of them lived on in the old weatherboard and iron house. And, for the time being, after they were married the sisters continued to share the house. Dingle had the two attics in the gable of the house, a cramped spaciousness all his own. They could hear him moving about up there for he was a heavy man and they often could hear his thick voice mumbling to and fro as he talked to the secret people in his secret world in the roof.

The sisters spent their time looking after their babies which had been born within a few weeks of each other. Every day when they had bathed the babies and were washed themselves and dressed in freshly ironed clothes – they were always washing and ironing – they went out from the dark ring of trees around the house into the sunshine and, crossing the road, they walked, brushing against hibiscus and lantana with their hips and thighs, up the hill to the shops. Joanna had a little pram but Deirdre carried her son, his dark fuzzy head nestled against the creamy skin of her plump neck. The sisters gazed at the things in the shops and they met people they had known all their lives and they showed off their lovely babies.

Everything was peaceful in the household except when the conversation turned, as it often did, to land prices and whether they should sell the house and the land. All round them the old houses had been sold and blocks of flats and two-storey townhouses with car parks instead of gardens were being built. Joanna longed for a modern house on one of the estates. She had magazines full of glossy pictures and often sat looking at them.

'Look at this electric kitchen, Deirdre,' she would say. 'Just look at all these cupboards fitting in to the walls!' But Deirdre wanted to stay in the house; as well as being fond of the place where she had always lived, she had a deep wish to go on with a continuation of something started years ago. Sometimes she pictured to herself the people who first built the house and she thought of them planting trees and making paths and as she trod the paths she rested on these thoughts. And of course the house with the big tangled garden was the only world Dingle could have. And the house did belong to all three of them.

'The value of the land's gone up again!' Joanna said at breakfast. 'Why don't we sell now and build? Oh, do let's!' Deirdre moved the milk jug and pushed aside the bread. 'I want to stay here,' she said.

How would Dingle be on a new housing estate where no one knew or understood him? She imagined him pressing the old tennis ball, which he thought contained happiness, on complete strangers. It was all right at the bowling club where he went sometimes to trim the lawns, they knew him there and would take the dirty old ball and thank him and then give it back. Sometimes Dingle lost his ball and Deirdre and Joanna, scolding, had to leave their housework and help him search for it in the fallen leaves beneath the overgrown pomegranates, and, in the fragrance of the long white bells of the datura, they parted stems and flowers searching for happiness for Dingle.

'What about Dingle?' Deirdre asked, her voice trembled. She was afraid Freddy, Joanna's neat quick husband, would insist they have a place of their own. Freddy and Joanna had more money, and in any case Joanna was entitled to her share of the house and land.

'There would be enough from the sale,' Spiro, Deirdre's husband said. He spoke slowly with a good-natured heaviness. They had to wait while he slowly chewed another mouthful. 'With his share, your fool of a brother could be very comfortable in some nice home.' Spiro did not mean to be unkind, Deirdre knew this, but she could not bear what he said. She felt they were all against her. More than anything she wanted to stay in the house and she wanted for Dingle to be able to stay but she and Spiro had no money with which to pay Joanna and Freddy their share. So Deidre said nothing, she got up from the table and started to go about her work and the talk was dropped for the time being.

Their lives went on as usual and the two sisters were kept busy with their babies.

One day Spiro came home in the middle of the afternoon. He walked straight through the kitchen and into the room which was their bedroom and he shut the door. The two sisters looked at each other and Deirdre put her baby down in his basket and went after her husband.

'He's not feeling well,' she said, coming back after a few minutes.

'Why? What's wrong?'

'Nothing much, but I think he's had words with the Boss. He's going to have a sleep.'

Joanna shrugged.

'There's nothing like a good sleep,' she said. 'We'd better keep quiet.'

'Yes, a good sleep,' Deirdre agreed. Mostly the two sisters agreed. Their mother, too, had been an agreeable woman; hard working and thrifty, she had wisdom too.

'Sisters give things to each other,' she said when Joanna wanted to sell her sequined party bag to Deirdre.

'Give the bag,' Mother said. 'Sisters don't buy and sell with each other. They share things. Sisters share.'

And she had left them the house to share, Dingle included, of course. But when Deirdre thought about it, how could she expect Joanna to give her her share of the house.

Deirdre's husband continued to stay at home. He seemed to step on plastic toys and lemons and he was bored with all the washing and ironing and the disorder brought about by the two babies. For though the sisters kept the shabby house clean, there was a certain untidiness which was comfortable but Deirdre, as Spiro stumbled crossly, began to see squalor everywhere. The verandas needed sweeping every day, paint peeled and fell in flakes and there were rusty marks. For some reason wheat was growing wild in the rough laundry tubs and they had to wash clothes in the bathroom. Joanna worked hard too but she complained and kept on wishing for a modern house. She reproached Deirdre.

Deirdre felt annoyed with Spiro for being at home all the time when she wanted to clean the house. As well as being annoyed she was worried that he might not have any work, and then how would they manage. She avoided her husband.

And then the two sisters began to quarrel over small things.

'If you don't want to make your bed,' Deirdre shouted at Joanna, 'at least close your door so the whole world needn't see what a pig sty your room is?'

'Who cares! Bossy Boots!' Joanna tossed her head, and their voices rose as they flung sharp words at each other. They moved saucepans noisily and scraped chairs and there was no harmony in their movements when they prepared the dinner.

Joanna began to do things for Deirdre's husband. She made tea for him in the middle of the long hot afternoon. She sat talking to him, her pretty head turned to one side as she gazed attentively while he replied in his slow speech. Deirdre saw that she sat there with her blouse still unfastened after feeding her baby. And it seemed to Deirdre that Spiro was watching Joanna and looking with admiration at her small white breasts which were delicately veined and firm with the fullness of milk.

Deirdre went out shopping alone.

'I'm leaving Robbie,' she called out to her husband. 'Watch him when he wakes, will you.'

She had several things to buy from the supermarket. It would have been wiser to ask Spiro to go with her. She took upon herself the burden of the shopping and in her present unhappiness she thought she wouldn't buy a Christmas tree.

The two sisters had taken some time to find husbands. Deirdre, nine years older than Joanna and with her straight-cut dull hair and sullen expression, had taken somewhat longer. Spiro had come just in time into Deirdre's life for the two sisters to be married on the same day.

Deirdre wished she could be alone with Spiro and persuade him to go back to his work before Christmas, even if only for half a day to make everything all right for after the holiday. But she knew he was a quiet man and proud, and besides, he was enjoying a kind of new discovery in her sister. Nothing like this had ever happened in the household before. Joanna's husband was deeply in love with his wife. He was always kind to Dingle and roguishly polite to

Deirdre, admired her baby and her cooking, but really he only cared about Joanna and their own baby daughter. Joanna took all his love, basking, cherished, she seemed to glow more every day with the love she had from Freddy and now here she was trying to attract her own sister's husband, as if she wanted both men to pay every attention to her.

Unhappiness and jealousy rose in Deirdre and she trembled as she put packages in her bag and she thought again she wouldn't bother to have a tree this year. But on the way home she passed a watered heap of Christmas trees sheltered from the sun by a canvas screen.

'How much are the trees?' she asked the boy.

'Dollar fifty,' he looked at her hopefully.

'I'll take one,' she said, sparing the money from her purse, wondering whether she should.

'Which'll you want?' He reached into the heap and shook out one tree after another till she chose one with a long enough stem. Slowly she dragged it home.

They put the tree in the hall, it seemed the best place for it though they had to squeeze by. It seemed to Deirdre when the tree was decorated with the little glittering treasures saved from their childhood that there was an atmosphere of peace in the tranquil depths of the branches, and, as she brushed against it, a fragrance which seemed to come from previous years soothed her. The corners of the rooms and the woodwork seemed as if smoothed and rounded, the brown linoleum and the furniture, polished for so many years, were mellow and pleasant to look upon because of this fragrance from the tree. She felt better and wondered why she had been so unhappy.

'I think I can smell rain,' she said, smiling as she stepped on to the back veranda. 'It must be raining somewhere.'

'Yes, there's weather coming up,' Freddy agreed and they paused to breathe in the sharp fragrance of rain-laden air. Later they played table tennis; the old boards creaked and the house seemed to shake but the contented babies and Dingle the Fool slept in spite of the noise.

For some reason Joanna had put on a stupid frock. It had no shoulder straps or sleeves and she kept missing the ball and spoiling the game because she kept tugging up her frock saying it was slipping down. And every time she missed the ball she dissolved into laughter and the two men laughed too and Deirdre noticed how her husband only looked at Joanna. Usually he was impatient if anyone played badly but tonight he was laughing with Joanna.

'Oh, I'm too tired to play any more.' Deirdre put her bat down suddenly.

'I'll take on the two men then,' Joanna cried. Deirdre wanted to shake Joanna, but she tried to control her anger, her voice trembled.

'No, Joanna,' she said as quietly as she could. 'I want to talk about the house.'

'Oh, Deirdre!' Joanna said. 'The agent was here again this morning while you were out, they're going to start building on the block next door quite soon. He promised us a really good price if only we'll sell!'

'Be quiet, Joanna!' Deirdre said. 'I want to say how a house has such history, such meaning. Places, especially houses are important, they matter.' Somehow she couldn't go on, she kept thinking about Dingle.

They had to wait, Spiro was speaking, his broken English more noticeable.

'It's what a person really wants that has meaning,' Spiro said slowly. 'For you Deirdre, this house. For Joanna, it is new house,' he shrugged his shoulders lazily. 'It is the wanting that matters,' he said. Deirdre's sallow face flushed a dull red.

'I know you and Freddy want a modern home of your own,' she said. 'We'll sell this place,' she forced out the words; she had been preparing them all evening.

'Oh, Deirdre!' Joanna hugged her sister. 'Shall we really!' She was shrill with excitement. 'Mr Rusk, you know, the agent, said our two acres could be a gold mine if only we'd sell now!'

'Oh, be quiet, Joanna!' Deirdre said, she couldn't stop thinking of Dingle. 'There's no more to be said,' she snapped. 'Sisters share,' her mother had said. Deirdre couldn't share Spiro with Joanna.

'We'll sell,' she made herself say it again.

'Oh, Deirdre!' Joanna hitched up her frock. 'Oh, we'll go on Sunday and look at the show houses on the Greenlawns Estate. Do let's!'

'Perhaps,' Deirdre said shortly. Joanna got out her magazines. 'Look at these kitchens.' She was showing her treasures to the two men long after Deirdre had gone, sleepless, to bed.

The two sisters sat together in the humid heat.

'I hope it'll be cooler on Christmas Day,' Joanna said.

They fed their babies and drank cold water, greedily taking turns to drink from a big white jug while their babies sucked.

Spiro was out. Deirdre felt comforted. He was driving a load of baled lucerne hay, it was only work for one day, but it was something. She leaned over to smile at Joanna's baby.

The air was heavy with the over-ripe mulberries fermenting and dropping, replenishing the earth. Soon the tree next door would be gone, the house had already been pulled down.

Dingle the Fool came in, his hands and face stained red.

'Oh, let us get some mulberries too!' Joanna laid her baby in her basket and Deirdre put her little son down quickly.

Soon the three of them were lost and laughing in the great tree, it was as big as a house itself.

They pushed in between the gnarled branches and twigs, climbing higher and deeper into the tree, pausing one after the other on the big forked branch where Dingle often slept on hot nights. All round them were green leaves, green light and green shade. For every ripe berry Deirdre picked, three more fell through her fingers. Splashing her face and shoulders, they dropped, lost to the earth. She felt restored in the tree, as if she could go on through the thick leaves and emerge suddenly in some magic place beyond. And, as she picked and ate the berries one after the other, she wondered why she had let things worry her so much.

'Here's a beauty!' Joanna cried. 'If only I could get it.' She leaned, cracking twigs, 'Oh, I missed it! Here's another.

Oh beauty!' The tree was full of their voices.

'Here's another!' Deirdre heard Joanna just above her and then Dingle slithered laughing beside her, smearing her white bare legs with the red juice. From above Joanna showered them both with berries and soon they were having a mulberry fight as they did when they were children together. Dingle could lose what little wits he had for joy.

Breathless and laughing they stood at last on the ground, stained all over with the stolen fruit.

'Anyone for a swim?' Spiro was back, he had the truck till the next day. His face widened with his good-natured smile as he saw them.

'Oh, I can't,' Deirdre said. And he remembered the mysterious things about the women after their childbirths and he was about to go off on his own.

'Wait for me! I'll come!' Joanna cried. 'Watch Angela for me, Deirdre, we'll not be long. Wait, Spiro! I'm coming!'

In the kitchen Deirdre stuck cloves into an onion and an orange. Slowly and heavily she began preparations for the Christmas cooking tomorrow. Reluctantly she greased a pudding basin. Sadness began again to envelop her. Joanna had scrambled up so quickly beside Spiro in the cabin of the truck. Deirdre tried to think of the mulberry fight instead.

Dingle came in, he had washed himself and flattened his colourless hair with water. He picked things up from the table and put them down, he examined the orange and the onion, he pulled out a clove and chewed it noisily.

'Oh, Dingle don't!' Impatiently Deirdre snatched them from him.

So then he began striking matches, one match after another. He watched the brief little flame with pleasure.

'Oh, Dingle, don't keep on wasting matches. Stop it!' Deirdre spoke sharply and then she tried to explain to him about the house being sold but he didn't seem to understand.

'You'll sleep in the doctor's nice bed,' she told him and tears came into her eyes as she spoke. Dingle came over to the table.

'Here,' he said to Deidre. 'You have this.' He held out the old tennis ball to his sister.

'No, No, Dingle,' Deirdre was impatient. 'Try and listen, we are selling the house – No! I don't want your old ball!'

'Go on!' Dingle interrupted. 'You have it, there's happiness inside.' He bounced the ball and gave it to her. She took it, her hand covered in flour.

'Thank you,' and she tried to give it back to him.

'No, you have it, keep it,' he insisted, his voice was thick and indistinct but Deidre always knew what he said. She refused to keep the ball. Flour fell on the floor.

Dingle drew a chair up to the table close to where she was working, he took her vegetable knife and began to cut the ball in half.

'No, Dingle, you Fool. Don't!' Deirdre cried out and she tried to take the knife, but Dingle had strength and he held on to the knife and began working it right into the ball.

'Dingle, you don't understand!'

'I understand,' he muttered, 'I understand, half each, you have half.'

He cut the ball and stared at the two empty halves of it. He looked at Deirdre and he looked at the two halves and, perplexed, he shook his head. He sat shaking his head and, as he realised the emptiness of the ball, his face crumpled and he cried, sobbing like a child except that he had white hair and a man's voice.

Deirdre had not seen him cry for years, she saw his mouth all square as he cried and it reminded her of Joanna's mouth when she cried and she could hardly bear to be reminded like this.

'Don't cry, Dingle. Please don't cry.' She spoke softly trying to comfort him. But it seemed there was nothing she could do.

In the night Joanna was thirsty and she got up to go for water. The hall was full of smoke.

'There's a fire!' she called, terrified in the smoke-filled darkness. 'The Christmas tree's burning! Deirdre! Quick! The house is on fire. Freddy! Spiro!'

The whole house seemed full of smoke and they couldn't tell which part was burning the most. They saved their babies and most of their clothes.

'Where is Dingle?' Deirdre hardly had breath to call out. Her eyes were blind with pain from the smoke.

Spiro tried to rush up to the attic but the heat and the burning timber falling forced him back out into the garden.

There was nothing anyone could do to save Dingle and

nothing to do to save the house. They stood in the ring of trees. The Norfolk pines, the cape lilacs, the jacarandas and the kurrajong and the great mulberry tree in the next garden were all lit up in the hot light of the flames. The noise of the fire seemed to make a storm in the trees. They stood, helpless little people, beside the big fire, their bare feet seeking out the coolness of fallen hibiscus flowers which had curled up slowly in their damp sad ragged dying on the grass.

There was nothing they could do to save Dingle. 'He will have suffocated from the smoke before the fire could reach him,' Spiro spoke slowly, he tried to comfort them. Deirdre saw his hands bursting with the burns he had received and she saw how he was hardly able to bear the pain of them and she persuaded him to go with a neighbour to have them bandaged. They all allowed themselves to be looked after, quietly, as if they couldn't understand what had happened.

And later, Deirdre, wandering in the half light of dawn while the others slept on the vinyl cushions in the lounge of the bowling club, went back to the smouldering soaked remains of the house. She half hoped her brother would be dead but how could she hope for him to be burned to death. In her unhappiness she felt the burden of his life. His life was too much for her but the pain of wishing him burned in the fire was even worse. She felt she must search in the remains of the house and was afraid of what she might find. It would be easier if he had slept on and on in the smoke as Spiro said he had.

She thought she saw him in the forked branch of the

mulberry tree. She paused, shivering, and hoped it was only his old washed-out shirt that was there, left behind after the mulberry fight. Dingle sometimes forgot his clothes and Deirdre often went about last thing at night gathering up his shoes and things.

She stood now and tried to see what was in the fork of the tree. She began, with hope and with fear to climb into the quiet branches, the cool damp leaves brushed her face and her arms and legs.

It was not just his shirt up there. Gently she woke him, empty match boxes fell as she shook him.

'Dingle, wake up!' He was asleep in the tree after all. Dingle the Fool stretched himself along the friendly branch. His face was as if stained with red tears. Deirdre hugged her brother clumsily, crying and kissing him. How could she have wished him dead?

'Another mulberry fight?' Dingle asked in his strange thick voice and he made a noise and Deirdre was unable to tell whether he was laughing or crying.

They thought they might as well choose a motel right on the sea front. They had only a short time to wait for their new houses to be ready. So every day they lay on the sand, even the babies sunbathed in their baskets.

'The quick brown fox,' Deirdre thought to herself as she watched Freddy put up the beach umbrella to make the best shade for Spiro who was still unwell after his burns.

Lazily they spent the days talking about nothing in particular and swimming and eating. They bought fried chicken and hamburgers to eat while watching television in the motel. There wasn't any point in wondering about the fire so they didn't talk about it.

Deirdre couldn't help thinking about Dingle. When she took him to the hospital he sat so awkwardly on the edge of the white bed. She wondered whatever could he do there. She went to the window.

'You can watch the road from here,' she said. Dingle got up and came to the window and obediently looked out at the corner of the road. There were no grass plots, Deirdre wished there was some grass and she could have asked if he could trim the edges. It was something he always enjoyed. She thought about him watching the empty street. What would he be doing now, Deirdre wondered. She watched Joanna and Freddy laughing in the sea. Joanna looked so happy, the green water curled handsomely round her lovely body. Deirdre envied Joanna, she envied her sister's innocence.

'The land's more valuable than ever with the house and sheds gone and on top there's all the insurance!' Deirdre seemed to hear Joanna's excited voice ringing, she envied her happiness but more enviable was her innocence. Joanna had never wished her brother burned to death.

'Where's that fool of a brother of yours?' Spiro often asked this question when he came in, sometimes he had something for Dingle, a cake or some apples, sometimes he wanted Dingle to help him move a heavy box or shift the load in his truck with him.

Everyone called Dingle a fool, their mother said he would give everything he had and people would take it.

Deirdre had taken everything from him, she had made

him give everything. Freddy and Joanna seemed hilarious in the water and Spiro, sitting with both hands bandaged, was laughing and laughing and all the time he watched Joanna.

'It's the wanting that really matters.' Spiro had said it himself.

Deirdre longed to talk about Dingle. She wanted to ask Spiro if he thought Dingle would be all right. She wanted comfort and reassurance but did not ask.

Near them on the beach was a bread-carter woman eating her lunch. She looked so carefree and sunburned and strong, Deirdre almost spoke to her.

'I have a brother – ' but she didn't. In a little while the bread carter would eat her last mouthful and be gone, taking with her her strength and vitality.

Deirdre lay back, she heard the sea come up the sand with a little sigh. Tears welled up under her closed eyelids. Joanna and Freddy came running from the water and Deirdre turned her face away so that they shouldn't see the tears spill over her cheeks.

INCIDENT IN THE HOTEL TANGIER

MATT CONDON

For three nights running I have sat here in the cocktail lounge of the Hotel Tangier and listened to a singer by the name of Kiki La Monde.

I am growing fond of Kiki. I have already purchased two of her home-recorded cassettes. I will buy another one tonight. If I come tomorrow night, I will buy a fourth.

Yes, I have had a little too much to drink. I make no excuses. I have perhaps become a little over enthusiastic about the Hotel Tangier's cocktail of the week – the Red Hound – the ingredients of which I have jotted down on the back of a palm-tree shaped drinks coaster for Gustave, back at the Lime Bar. I think Gustave will find a drink called the Red Hound somewhat amusing.

I have found, though, that the Red Hound actually complements Kiki La Monde. That Kiki and the Hound somehow work together in a way I have yet to understand.

She takes away the bitterness of the grapefruit juice. And the Hound brings a certain warmth to Kiki's rendition of 1930s cocktail lounge favourites.

I cannot tell you how it stirs me when she closes her eyes and sings that she's daddy's little girl.

During the break in Kiki's set I ponder this theory of drinks going with people, just as certain wines belong to individual dishes. Certainly Gustave would not be Gustave without vodka and lime juice. When I think of my business partner Lloyd I instantly see a tumbler of Scotch on the rocks. And what of my ex-wife Margaret? What of her? She had started out as champagne, and ended as, well, a cold spumante. But I am just being vindictive. She is probably in the arms of someone else right now, as supple as a Grange. The Grange that slipped through my fingers.

I have amused myself. I write this down on one of the cardboard fronds of the coaster.

'I'll remember youuuuuuu, alllllwayyyyysssss . . .'

I am astonished that the other patrons of the bar do not recognise Kiki La Monde's versatility. Granted, her orchestral backing music is pre-recorded. But her flute and saxophone work, interlaced with her voice, is nothing short of astonishing. I am offended for her at the ill-attention of my fellow drinkers. Kiki is not a canvas *backdrop* to their idle chatter and boorish flirting. Kiki is not *furnishing* in the dull drama of their evenings.

'Bravo!' I shout, clapping loudly.

The bar goes silent. You can hear the shift of beer nuts and Indian split peas.

But what the hell. I am here on the Gold Coast in the

Hotel Tangier being pursued by the Red Hound and I am falling in love with a nineteen-year-old lounge singer called Kiki La Monde and life for once is good because it is not my life, it is the life of me as a conference-goer on the Gold Coast where I can be anything or anyone I like.

It is what I love about the Gold Coast and why I did not hesitate in registering for the South-East Asian Small Traders Conference. It will bring no business. It will produce no valuable contacts. But there are times, in life, when you have to take leave of yourself for a while. When you're so sick of being *you* that you have to hang up the old Back in Five Minutes sign and take leave for a while.

There is no better place to do this than on the Gold Coast. Nothing is real. Nobody is who they seem. This is how I like it.

I did not tell my father of the conference. I have never told him anything about my business, not even over golf. My father has dealt in stocks and shares all his life. Not the little fish, but the major stocks that hold up the world economy. He also has a sideline in Australian wheat and wool. My father trades millions of sacks and bundles of wool at any given hour. How, then, could I tell him I make money from mass produced trinkets out of Asia? Against my father's huge dealings, I am a Lilliput business. I deal with little factories and little items that would fit into the pockets of my father's golf bag.

I chose the Hotel Tangier for my conference accommodation because I had a sudden penchant for some North African exotica. I am tickled by the staff in their long and flowing robes, and the fez of the concierge. I have recommended to management that they provide a fez in each room, just as other hotels supply bathrobes and complimentary personal hygiene items. They seem interested in the idea.

I could have booked into a facsimile of Hawaii, or New York, or Munich, or Santorini. All these options were available. But it was, ultimately, the fez that sold it to me.

My business partner Lloyd is staying with the other conference-goers, two blocks down in Hong Kong. I have attended enough of these things, however, to learn the golden rule of the conference – always avoid the other people who actually go to them.

I established this maxim early when, as a young man, I was sent to Port Macquarie on a confectionery conference. There was an unsavoury drama, which I won't go into here, involving a Smarties representative from Glenelg. And innumerable tiffs and threats of actual violence between sales reps of Violet Crumbles and Turkish Delights. This incident is still referred to in confectionary circles. This is what it comes down to, no matter what area of life you move in. Politics. Rank. Teams. One-upmanship. No one, as far as I know, has come up with a more violently imaginative use of a Turkish Delight. As far as I know.

I sup on another Red Hound and close my eyes as Kiki La Monde does a reedy but very plausible imitation of Ella Fitzgerald. I applaud warmly. I wonder if there are other singers in smaller bars than that of the Hotel Tangier imitating Kiki La Monde.

'Encore!'

Someone tosses a pretzel in my direction.

I am not against the notion of the conference. Not at all. They have given me much over the years. My friend and occasional golfing partner, Olivier, says he goes to at least one conference annually for a personal and private nervous breakdown which, in the end, he can write off on tax.

In fact, Olivier's method is quite unique and has been passed on, with success, to other close friends. He shuts himself in his room, draws the blinds, and plays, over and over, the video of the film *Titanic*. He starts the video not at the beginning, and well past the 'I'm king of the world' quip. He starts it when the ship first strikes trouble then, in the dark, listens to the disaster at close to full volume. He says this brings on his breakdown and excises his stress in a more economical fashion. 'If you've been to the bottom,' he says, 'there's only one way to go.'

I have learnt much, also, about human behaviour at the conference. I know that people can fall in love very quickly when removed from the routine of their own environment. I have seen astounding couplings that would never have been considered beyond the borders of the conference. I have seen people fall into frenetic affairs by virtue of being paired with a surname alphabetically close to their own. Over time I have considered this method of mating – the A's and B's stick together, the C's and D's. It's as good a way of getting together as any. I don't want to think of the problems involved amongst the WXYZ's. But this is in hindsight. In the moment it is insanity. Then again, I have never found it difficult to fall in love.

Kiki La Monde is moving around the bar with her satchel of cassettes. I admire her confidence. I admire her self-belief. I admire her young cleavage.

'Good evening,' she says sweetly, approaching me.

'Well good evening.'

'Would you care to buy . . .'

But I am ahead of her. I have the wallet open.

'Twenty-five dollars?'

'Yes,' she says, surprised.

'I love your work,' I say, smiling, and I wonder how many millions of men around the world have said 'I love your work' to a woman in the past few hours.

'Why thank you,' she says, passing me the cassette of Kiki La Monde's 'Warm Evenings'.

I tuck the cassette in the pocket of my sports jacket. I am feeling considerably warm inside. No matter that Kiki has brought her wares to my couch three nights in a row and still does not recognise me from the night before. This is a place where everything starts afresh at the dawn of each day. That's another thing I love about the Gold Coast.

'Would you like a drink?' I ask, but she has already gone.

I order a final Red Hound and notice Kiki in conversation with the barman. They are both looking at me discreetly. I smile and give a small wave. Kiki waves back. I look away coolly, and hum a riff from 'Always'.

I finish my drink and leave the bar. Kiki has finished for the evening. The barman is polishing his glasses. I knock into a plastic palm tree on the way out but don't think anyone notices. I stand unsteadily at the elevator and see my distorted face in the brass plate behind the elevator buttons.

I sit in the dark on the verandah of my room overlooking the beach and am refreshed by the sea breeze. It is then that I commit the second crime of conferences – never go swimming in the hotel pool whilst drunk.

I don't forsee any drama. I am not, after all, at the official conference hotel with its own offical conference pool and spa where official conference-goers could be, at that very moment, slipping hands into each other's swimming trunks beneath a screen of bubbles from the spa jets. I am in the Hotel Tangier, heading down in the lift in my fluffy white Hotel Tangier bathrobe to a pool shimmering beneath rustic red and white brick Moroccan colonnades. I tap my bare foot on the lift carpet. I belch a grapefruit-inspired belch.

I am alone in the pool. I float on my back and think of Kiki La Monde and see her emerging naked from the dark wood sauna in a fine haze of steam and the scent of pine needles.

I gently knock my head against the end of the pool, right myself, and, incredibly, she is there, at the end of the pool, in her tight black Kiki La Monde cocktail dress.

'Kiki,' I say, and her name echoes off the brick arches. 'Kiki, iki, iki, ki, ki, i.'

'May I join you?'

She doesn't wait for my answer. She simply slips off her dress and enters the pool in nothing but a pale pink G-string. She swims slowly towards me, loops her hands around my neck, and kisses me gently on the neck.

'Kiki,' I say. I do not comprehend the situation. I have a vague and somewhat unformed notion that it has to do with the number of copies of 'Warm Evenings' I have purchased.

She leads me into the spa where I sit uncomfortably close to a jet. I am rigid, not with fear, but with surprise at the infinite turns that life takes.

'I love your work,' I say woodenly. Kiki La Monde plays with my knobbly knees under the water.

'So how long have you been with Sony?'

I do not hear her. The hairs on my legs and thighs are erect and tingling in the seething water.

'Pardon?'

'Sony. How long have you been with them?'

Sony. Sony. This word registers with me somewhere. I try to reach through the fog of the Red Hounds and retrieve it. It takes several long minutes but it finally comes to me. I remember the Welcome to the Hotel Tangier sandwich board in the foyer. Sony. Sony. It is a gross case of mistaken identity. I have accidentally been consumed by another conference.

'About five years,' I say.

And Kiki La Monde slides both hands into the legs of my complimentary Hong Kong Handover 97 swimming trunks.

MERMAID BEACH

JULIE SIMPSON

One afternoon in January, her day's work done, Antonia takes her sailing boat out from Wall-Eyed Beach to explore some other small bays and beaches along the coast. Armed with a picnic in a thermal bag for herself and Starpaws, and some scraps for the seagulls and mutton birds, she feels perfectly content.

A good breeze is up and her sails are full. She skims along until she notices a beach she hasn't seen before, half-hidden in a deep curve in the cliff-line. Dropping anchor she lowers herself and Starpaws into the dinghy and rows to shore, her fair crest whipping up over her head while her dog's soft ears stream in the breeze.

Sitting high on a wind-sculpted rock after lunch, Antonia watches a platoon of soldier crabs marching up the sand. Crabs are very neat in everything they do, eight legs keep the beat as each slips sideways through the shallows, pincers clicking air like tiny castanets.

The dog's sudden barking startles Antonia from her reverie. Starpaws has obviously found something exciting. In the lee of the rock where the girl sits someone has modelled a life-sized mermaid flat in the sand. Captivated by her wistful smile and heavy-lidded eyes peering out from under her hair, long lines etched straight into the sand, Antonia notices the mermaid is wearing a necklet of star-shaped limpet shells and her tail sweeps to the right in a delicate swirl. A pattern of scales has been pressed into it with the top of a scallop shell and her outstretched arms reveal two perfectly circular breasts tipped with red berries – she has a most generous personality.

Antonia decides to make her a merman for company, a fine fellow with flowing seaweed locks, a necklace of cone shells and a starfish belly button. His tail twists in the opposite direction while echoing the swirl of his mate's. His arms, too, are outstretched, and in one hand he carries a perfect cuttlefish as a gift. They make a handsome pair.

At five o'clock, feeling rather elated, Antonia whistles her dog and sails home.

On her next afternoon off she sails back to Mermaid Beach, as she now calls it, to see if anything has happened to the sand sculptures. To her delight she finds two new mermaids cavorting about her merman, each with a different face. One is very sophisticated, with piled-up seagrass hair adorned with bright birds' feathers and pebble earrings and her eyes are wide with matchstick eyelashes. The other is dreamy, with eyes shut in half moons. She wears a seaweed scarf and a scallop shell on each breast. The original one with the inviting arms has been tenderly restored and Antonia's merman is carrying a trident made from an old barbecue fork instead of the cuttlefish she gave him.

She models two more mermen for the other girls: a jaunty one with a Dali moustache for the sophisticated mermaid and one with Botticelli curls made out of bubbleweed for the dreamy one. She gives him a bouquet of star shells and he looks remarkably like Barrie until she savagely changes his hairstyle.

Once a week for the next month she visits Mermaid Beach. She can't resist it. And after each visit her dreams become more vivid. At work she spends a lot of time thinking about the unknown sculptor on the beach. It has to be a man, there is something about the mermaids that tells her so. Perhaps it's the idealised shape of their bosoms, placed up too high, as men are apt to do in many forms of art.

In the shelter of the great sloping rock the sand-sculpted family multiplies. Merchildren appear: little sprats and mackerels dance between the adult couples trailing strips of Neptune's necklace attached to fish skeletons, crabs or the delicate mosaic centres of sea urchins. One cradles a plastic Ronald McDonald figurine that has washed up among the natural detritus along the shore.

Antonia is modelling a seahorse for a merchild to ride on when she feels eyes upon her. She freezes, the sand dropping from her hand, while Starpaws growls a warning. A shadow falls across her work and, without a word, a young man drops to his knees beside her and begins to sculpt a flying fish. Refusing to be flummoxed by his confidence and style, she adds another. He a third. Soon a flight of fishes arches like a rainbow over their merry merfamily.

He sculpts a sun, she a moon as the sand flies about them in a frenzy of creative joy. They have not spoken a word. At the end of the afternoon fish, birds, dolphins, starfish, crabs – all the sea creatures they can think of – sport with their mermaids, mermen and merchildren.

Just before five the young man makes his last piece for the day, a big plump heart, right in front of Antonia as she sits back on her heels watching him, with one arm around her dog. The young man is strong but gentle, with tousled dark curls and eyes deep green as the evening sea. His silence is golden.

He looks up at her and then writes with a stick in the sand:

My name is Benedict
I can't hear or speak but I love you XX

Antonia stares directly at the sand in front of her as Benedict, flushed with embarrassment, strides off along the beach.

The terror of any form of commitment leaves Antonia rigid but their sand sculptures still dance with joy, they have no way of losing it. As she looks from one to another, reabsorbing their magic and blinking through tears, she struggles to make a decision. Finally she jumps up and runs after Benedict, waving her arms. He stops, turns back as she writes in large letters just above the tide line:

Let me try. Antonia.

Benedict smiles as she tentatively adds an X.

THE ABSOLUTE AUTHORITY ON EVERYTHING

DEREK HANSEN

Always check your gear before fishing.
Look for dubious knots and chafed line.
If there's a weakness, the fish will find it.

Albert Arthurton Eversleigh, tall, balding, big boned and angular, retired the day he turned fifty. He sold his studio in North Sydney without any trouble at all. There were no shortage of buyers. Albert's photographic studio was the best equipped in Australia.

If you wanted to shoot cars, you went to Albert's. You didn't have to spend days battling reflections there. Albert understood the problems, and his egg-shaped studio overcame most of them. If you wanted to shoot animals, you went there. His was the only studio with proper kenneling. If you wanted to shoot people, you went there. If you wanted to shoot anything, you went to Albert's.

Albert's studio had everything, and it more than made up for the shortfalls in Albert's talent.

So he was always busy and he charged accordingly. He sold his studio for one and a half million dollars. Everyone was stunned by the price. Except Albert.

'Quality has its price,' said Albert. 'You can never pay too much for it.'

Albert sold his Hasselblads.

'The camera that turned the business on its head,' he said, and was contemptuous of anyone who used anything else.

He sold his Nikons.

'Any professional who uses anything else is unprofessional,' he said, and was contemptuous of all those photographers who used Pentax, Canon, Minolta.

He sold his old Leica.

'It's the only camera to do pack shots with,' he said. 'It's the lens.' And he was contemptuous of every pack shot taken with any camera other than his own. 'Not sharp,' he'd say, and walk away.

Albert's studio was always popular, but Albert never was. When he said he was retiring to live in Fiji, they said good luck to his face and good riddance behind his back. And they looked forward to life without the AAE.

For years Albert never understood why they called him the AAE. He thought it was a sign of respect in an industry that loved to use initials. The definite article made it somehow special, a quasi title, a nod to his pre-eminence. He sat in the toilet one day and learned otherwise.

'I thought you said you'd never use the AAE again,' one urinater said.

'I've cracked the secret,' said the other. 'Volunteer nothing,' he said. 'Keep your mouth shut. Then the Absolute Authority on Everything has absolutely nothing to be an absolute authority on.'

Albert went home and told his wife what he'd heard. She was very understanding.

Albert took very many photos of very many beautiful women. Very many beautiful bare bottoms, and very many beautiful bare breasts. Yet he remained ever faithful to his little cream puff, as he often called her.

'Why bother?' he said. 'None of them can cook, keep house, clean fish, or do anything useful. Soon their tits and bums will sag and they still won't be able to cook, keep house, clean fish, etcetera, etcetera.'

Albert took his wife with him to Fiji. Albert wanted to retire to Fiji. His wife never said if she did and he never asked.

'When a woman loves a man,' said Albert, 'she'll go with him wherever he wants to go. And my little dumpling adores me. Yes, indeed.' He often called his wife his little dumpling, too.

Among the Fijian women she didn't look quite so plump or plain. But not everyone on the island was Fijian. Albert bought the eleventh house on the eleventh block, on the one kilometre by one-and-a-half kilometre island of Naviti Lau.

'Naviti,' people said to him when they discovered the

name of the island he was retiring to. 'In the Yasawas. Very nice.'

'Are you mad?' Albert would reply. 'Not Naviti. Naviti Lau. In the Lau Group, on the eastern side. Why would anyone want to go to the Yasawas? Crawling with bloody tourists. Might be all right for you, but not me. No, if you know anything at all about Fiji, you keep as far away from the western side as you can. Only fools and madmen go there.'

And people would grit their teeth behind fixed smiles, ponder the inequities of the laws relating to justifiable homicide, and vow never to speak to the Absolute Authority on Everything ever again.

On the second night after they set up house in their new home on Naviti Lau, the island manager held a welcoming party. The six home owners then in residence on the island also came. They came curious to meet their new neighbours. Four families were from the USA, one from Germany, and one also from Australia. They were all, without exception, very wealthy with interesting stories to tell. Albert never gave them a chance.

'I think we did rather well there,' Albert said afterwards to his little pumpkin. He often called her his little pumpkin. 'They're very rich. In my book that makes them very smart. You don't get rich by being stupid. Still, I managed to put them right on a few things.'

Hermann the German, tall, thin and stork-like, told Albert about his passion for cars. He told him about his Mercedes Benz collection. His 1929 seven-litre supercharged 38/250SSK roadster, his 1935 170S cabriolet staff car, said to have been used by Göring. His 1955 300 SL gullwing. His new Mercedes Benz 500 convertible, with roll-bar which flips up automatically as soon as any wheel lifts off the ground.

'Never been one for the three-pointed star,' said Albert. 'Can't see anything in them. No soul, that's the problem. Might be all right for you Germans, all that soulless efficiency, but I'm a Jaguar man myself. Now there's a car. You'd have been better off collecting Jaguars. The SS 100. First production sportscar to do one hundred miles per hour. The D-type. Frogs should have given Le Mans away when they stopped racing. Out of respect. The E-type.' Etcetera, etcetera, etcetera.

By the time Albert had finished Hermann wanted to run him over with his 1929 roadster, his 1935 cabriolet, his 1955 gullwing, his 500 convertible. But he just smiled and gritted his teeth.

Marvin the Californian, short, overweight and Jewish, offered to help him get a boat built. Marvin had a twin-hull, twin 140 hp outboard, fly-bridge cruiser built for him in Suva.

'They're ideal for the short, steep chop and shallow reef waters around here,' Marvin said.

'Wouldn't have a cat on my mind let alone on the waters around here,' Albert said. 'That short chop pounds up on the flat area between the two hulls. Do in my knee cartilages in the first week.'

'They'll make you a single hull,' said Marvin bravely. 'Fijian style, long and narrow gutted, shallow draught.'

'I wouldn't go out in it,' said Albert. 'Certainly not in these waters. Hopeless in a following sea. Takes waves over the stern. Why would anybody want a boat that takes waves over the stern? Have to be mad to have a boat like that. No, I'm bringing over a Blackfin 28. It's a Queensland boat. Perfect for here.'

'You'll be up for import duty. Sixty percent,' warned the manager, at thirty, the youngest present by twenty years.

'It always costs to do things right,' said Albert. 'I never compromise. When you see it, you'll understand what you should have bought.'

Marvin smiled and gritted his teeth.

Brewer the Australian, built like an ex-wrestler, offered to take him fishing.

'Your wife says you like to try your luck fishing,' said Brewer.

'Luck's got nothing to do with it,' said Albert.

'Caught a seventeen kilo dog-tooth tuna last week,' Brewer said. 'In the main channel. Put out live mullet and drifted.'

'That's cheating,' said Albert. 'Never use live bait, myself. Too easy. Might be all right for you, but good fishermen use lures. Not store-bought rubbish, either. I make all my lures myself. I reckon if you can't make your own lures, you don't deserve the fish.'

'Really,' said Brewer.

'Absolutely,' said the Absolute Authority on Everything. 'I hold the six-kilo Australian record for dog-tooth. Forty-nine point two kilos.'

'Congratulations,' said Brewer.

'Rightly so,' said Albert. 'What say I show you? Never too late to learn. Why don't we take your boat out tomorrow, an hour before dusk? If you want real fish, the ones worth bothering with, they hit just as the sun goes down.'

'Look forward to it,' said Brewer.

The party broke up shortly after ten.

'Early nights the go around here?' said Albert.

'Not normally,' said the manager.

The next evening Albert, Marvin and Brewer went fishing. Albert brought the lures. Mullet pattern with big bibs to take them deep. Others with black or brown backs, mackerel stripes and silver bellies, that swam two metres below the surface. He brought his high-speed lures. With black skirts, green skirts, yellow skirts, and his favourites with red, orange, yellow and silver skirts.

Brewer guided his boat up and down the channel in the figure eight pattern Albert insisted upon.

'Any moment now,' said Albert.

'Strike!' yelled Marvin.

'You take it!' yelled Brewer.

'Keep the tip up,' advised Albert.

'Look at all the line it's taking,' yelled Marvin.

'Yahooo!' yelled Brewer.

'Don't wind against the drag,' advised Albert. 'Twists the line.'

'What do you think?' asked Marvin.

'Yellowfin tuna,' said Brewer.

'Walu,' said Albert. 'Spanish mackerel. About twenty kilos.'

Five minutes later the exhausted fish appeared off the stern.

'Walu,' said Brewer.

'Told you,' said Albert. 'I'll get the gaff.'

'Go for the shoulder,' said Brewer.

'Head shot's better,' said Albert. 'Doesn't spoil the fish.' Albert expertly gaffed the mackerel in the thick part of the head and lifted it aboard. It flapped and splashed and sprayed the boat with its blood.

'Wow!' said Marvin. 'What a beauty!'

'Twenty-five, maybe twenty-six kilos,' said Brewer.

'Twenty kilos,' said Albert.

It weighed in at twenty point five.

'Always call a touch under,' said Albert. 'Then you're never made to look a fool afterwards.'

Brewer gritted his teeth.

'That nine kilo gear is a little light for here,' said Brewer.

'Not in the hands of an expert,' said Albert, as he fitted a small black-backed, white-bellied, skirted lure to the trace.

'As you wish,' said Brewer.

'I'll run it short down the middle,' said Albert. 'It'll be the next one to go off.'

'Want to bet on that?' asked Marvin. 'We've got four other rods out. That only gives you one chance in five.'

'One hundred bucks,' said Albert.

'You're on!' said Marvin and Brewer. They would take their winnings with glee.

'Strike!' yelled Marvin.

'Told you,' said Albert. 'You owe me fifty dollars each.'

'Catch it first,' said Brewer, between gritted teeth.

The line screamed off the reel.

'You won't stop it,' said Brewer hopefully. 'You're too light.'

'Wahoo,' said Albert. 'About thirty kilos. Run parallel.'

'Okay,' said Brewer.

'There,' said Albert, 'It's done its dash. One big run and they're history. Back up to it.'

'Okay,' said Brewer.

'Not too fast,' said Albert.

'Okay,' said Brewer.

'Just watch the tip,' said Albert.

'Okay,' said Brewer. He backed up, not too fast, watching the tip. The wahoo, as Albert had said, had done its dash. It lay in the water just waiting to die, its colours reprising the sunset.

'Goddamn! Look at the size of it,' said Marvin.

'I'll get the gaff,' said Brewer.

'Head shot,' said Albert.

'Head shot,' said Brewer, gritting his teeth.

They caught four more fish. Neither Brewer nor Marvin had ever caught that many fish before. Brewer caught another dog-tooth. It went twenty-nine kilos. It dwarfed the dog-tooth he'd caught on live bait.

'What are we going to do with all this fish?' asked Marvin.

'Eat some, freeze the rest,' said Brewer.

'Better just keep the small ones and give the big ones to the Fijians,' said Albert.

'Why?' asked Marvin.

'Ciguatera,' said Albert. 'Shouldn't eat any reef fish longer than your arm. Don't you know that? Ciguatera poisoning is deadly. Might be all right for you, but I won't touch them. Not the big ones. Be mad to do that.'

'Of course,' said Brewer.

'I'll get my little cream puff to fillet them,' said Albert. 'Then drop it round to you.'

'Your wife fillets your fish!' said Marvin.

'Best filleter I've ever seen. Taught her myself. Cuts closer to the bone than a surgeon,' said Albert.

'Even so,' said Brewer.

'My little pudding worships me,' said Albert. 'When a woman loves a man, there's nothing she won't do for him.'

'How does she put up with him?' Marvin asked Brewer, when Albert had gone.

That night the six home owners in residence gathered once more at the manager's house. The AAE and his wife were not invited.

'What have you done to us?' demanded Brewer.

'We had no idea,' said the manager.

'You're going to have to do something about it,' said Marvin.

'Yes, yes, yes,' said the other home owners in residence.

'But what can I do?' asked the manager.

'That's your problem,' said Hermann.

Fortunately for the home owners in residence, their homes on Naviti Lau were not their only homes. Marvin and his fellow Americans took their families back to America. Hermann returned to his Mercedes Benz collection. Brewer returned to Australia. As they moved out, other home owners moved back in.

'You've missed the best part of the year,' said Albert to the latest arrivals. 'The summer months are no good.'

'Too hot,' he said.

'Cyclones,' he said.

'No,' he said, 'best you go back where you came from and come again in March. Fishing's better then, as well.'

'We always come this time of year,' they said. 'And we enjoy ourselves.'

'Some people never learn,' said Albert. 'My little pumpkin and I are off back to Australia for summer.'

'Goodbye, and good luck,' they said to his face. 'Good riddance,' they said behind his back.

'Good God!' they said to the manager. 'You're going to have to do something about that man.'

'What can I do?' he asked.

'That's your problem,' they said.

'Hello?' said Brewer, 'Anyone here?' Only one light was on in the bar. It was bravely held up by a miniature Johnnie Walker in top hat, red coat and white trousers. The bulb was forty watt and the shade had yellowed with age. It lit Johnnie, showing the mend in his broken leg, but nobody else.

'Not so loud!' hissed a voice. 'Welcome back.'

'We don't want anyone to know we're here,' hissed another voice.

'Don't want someone to know we're here, more like,' whispered another.

'Oh dear,' said Brewer. 'So it's come to this?'

The manager flashed a torch towards him.

'Over here,' he said. 'I'll get you a beer.'

'Last night we were told to throw away all our photos of Naviti Lau,' said Marvin. 'None of us, according to Albert, know the first thing about taking pictures in the tropics. Albert did new ones for us.'

'We all had to get up at five,' said Hermann. 'And stand around on the beach until it was our turn to be photographed.'

'Dawn light,' said Marvin. 'Only time to shoot.'

'We've all got to get new trays on our Suzuki four-wheel drives,' said the manager. 'We've all got steel. Albert has heavy duty alloy. Ours will rust out. Albert's won't.'

'I ran into some people back in Sydney,' said Brewer. 'They know our friend.'

'Not Albert Arthurton Eversleigh,' said Marvin.

'The same,' said Brewer.

'And?' asked Hermann.

'There's no hope for us,' said Brewer.

'Why?' asked Marvin.

'They have a name for him,' said Brewer. 'The AAE.'

'The AAE?' asked the manager.

'The Absolute Authority on Everything,' said Brewer.

'Good Lord,' said Marvin.

'Good heavens,' said Hermann.

'Good grief,' said the manager.

'He's dropped off more fish,' the manager's wife said. 'A whole yellowfin, and his wife's recipes for sushi.'

'Give it to the Fijians,' said the manager. 'One more piece of raw tuna and I'll puke.'

'The Fijians don't want it. They have enough,' said the manager's wife. 'He went there first.'

'The owners?'

'Their freezers are full. Walu, wahoo, yellowfin, dogtooth, trevally and Maori wrasse. Doesn't that man ever come home empty handed?' she asked.

'Apparently not,' said the manager. 'He's something of an authority on fishing.'

'An absolute authority,' his wife said. 'You're going to have to do something about him.'

'What can I do?' he asked.

'That's your problem,' she said.

'This island would starve without me,' Albert said to the owner-prospect. Despite the manager's careful shepherding, Albert had found him and his pretty, blonde wife.

'Really?' said the prospect.

'Oh yes,' said Albert. 'It costs a fortune to fly food in from Suva, so I keep all the owners supplied with fish. Very grateful they are too. Like fish, do you?'

'Not really,' said the prospect's wife.

'Oh you'll soon get a taste for it,' said Albert. 'Don't eat fish here, there's no point coming. I'll keep you supplied. Tell me what you like best, I'll catch it for you.'

'We'll keep that in mind,' said the owner-prospect.
'Bye for now,' said Albert.
'Goodbye and good luck fishing,' he said to his face.
'Luck has nothing to do with it,' said Albert.
'Well,' said the manager. 'Ready to sign?'
'That man. Does he come here often?' asked the prospect.
'Only once a year,' said the manager. 'For nine months.'
'We'll think about it,' said the prospect.

Over the next twelve months the company sold two more homes on two more blocks of land. They'd budgeted on selling ten. They only sold those because the Absolute Authority on Everything and his little dumpling were back in Sydney.

Worse, three existing home owners put their homes up for sale. Worse still, the remaining home owners began to come less frequently. And they stayed for shorter periods. The company lost money on sales. It lost money on the little store it ran, the little restaurant it ran, the little bar it ran, and on its refuelling bay.

'You're going to have to do something,' the company raged.

'What can I do?' asked the manager.

'That's your problem,' said the company. 'If you can't solve it, we'll get somebody who can.'

'What can I do?' asked the manager, as they sat in the darkness of the bar.

'Something might turn up,' said Marvin. 'We might get lucky. He might fall overboard.'

'We couldn't get that lucky,' said Brewer.

'Why not?' asked Hermann. 'It happens all the time in the North Sea. Fishing can be very dangerous. Particularly when the fisherman fishes alone.'

'Interesting,' said Marvin.

'Very interesting,' said Brewer.

'I'll look into it,' said the manager.

'Isn't it dangerous, fishing alone?' asked the manager, as Albert prepared for another day's slaughter.

'It is for some,' said Albert. 'But not for me. If it was dangerous I wouldn't do it. A man would be a fool to do it, if it was dangerous. What are you suggesting? Are you suggesting I'm a fool?'

'You're not a fool,' said the manager.

'No, I'm not,' said the Absolute Authority on Everything, and he showed him why.

'See this,' said Albert. 'I invented it myself. Anyone who fishes alone without one of these is off his head.' Attached to the side of the centre console was a small version of a fire hose reel.

'It takes twenty metres of line,' said Albert. Attached to the line was a harness that fitted over the shoulders and around the stomach. Albert fitted it to the manager.

'Now walk to the stern,' he said.

'Hey!' said the manager. 'It's spring loaded.'

'Of course,' said Albert, 'only a fool would have it any other way. If it wasn't on a spring, I'd be tripping over it all day.'

'Clever,' said the manager.

'Brilliant,' said Albert.

'Doesn't the harness get in the way, you know, when you're catching a fish?' asked the manager.

'Are you mad?' asked Albert. 'Of course not. I designed it. I told you that. You don't listen. It goes under my spray jacket. See? The carabina goes through this vent in the back and clips on here.'

'Brilliant,' said the manager.

'Now you're learning,' said Albert.

'No go,' said the manager, as Johnnie Walker once more kept them company in the bar. He told Brewer, Marvin and Hermann all about Albert's safety line. 'The man's safer at sea than he is on dry land.'

'The man is impossible,' said Marvin.

'Impossible,' said Hermann.

'Dear God,' said Brewer. 'We have to do something about that man.'

'But what can we do?' said the manager.

Fate lent a hand. Hermann got lucky. He caught a huge shark. They were taking pictures of it hanging off the scales at the end of the jetty when Albert brought his Blackfin in.

'At the end of the day, it's just a shark,' said Albert scathingly. 'Tell them.' He turned to his wife who'd brought the Suzuki down to pick him up and gut his fish.

'They know what it is, Albert,' she said.

'It may just be a shark to you, Albert. But it's the biggest fish anyone's ever caught off Naviti Lau,' the manager said.

'Five hundred kilos of angry tiger shark,' said Marvin.

'Angry?' said Albert. 'They're like hauling in a sack of wet concrete.'

'Just look at it,' said Brewer. 'I think Hermann deserves a trophy.'

'A trophy!' said Albert. 'But it's just a shark.'

'I agree,' said the manager. 'I think we should all put in for a trophy.'

'For a shark?' asked Albert.

'For the biggest fish ever caught off Naviti Lau,' said the manager.

'Biggest by a long shot,' said Marvin. 'Now come on, Albert, no sour grapes.'

'But it's just a shark,' said Albert. 'It doesn't compare with my sixty-two kilo walu on six kilo test. That takes skill.'

'It's also a bloody sight smaller than Hermann's shark,' said Brewer, enjoying himself. 'And that's what takes the prize. In my book, the man who catches the biggest fish is the best fisherman. Always been that way. Be mad to think otherwise. Right, Marvin?'

'Right,' said Marvin.

'Right,' said the manager.

'But it's just a shark,' said Albert.

'Perhaps you should give Albert a chance to catch a bigger shark,' said his wife. 'If there's going to be a trophy.'

They all looked at her.

'That's right,' said Albert. He gave his wife a look that fell just short of admiration.

'A competition?' asked the manager.

'Great idea,' said Brewer.

'A championship,' said Albert. 'With a trophy. Count me in. What are the rules?'

'What do you mean rules?' asked the manager.

'A championship has to have rules,' said Albert. 'Otherwise people can cheat.'

'For instance?' asked Brewer.

'No burley,' said Albert.

'No live bait,' said Albert.

'Nothing over sixty kilo test,' said Albert.

'Can't agree with that,' said Marvin.

'Me neither,' said Brewer.

'The competition, Albert,' said the manager, 'is to catch the biggest fish. Not the biggest fish on a lure. Agreed?'

'Agreed,' said Marvin and Brewer and Hermann.

'All right,' said Albert. 'If you want to behave like new chums on a ten dollar charter, you can. But if I'm going to do it, I'm going to do it right. I'll use lures. You use what you like. Won't make any difference. Order the trophy. Just make sure they spell my name right.'

'Albert Arthurton Eversleigh,' said the manager. 'AAE'.

'By the way,' said Albert. 'I'll need a week to get organised. And I'll need a deck hand. Can't catch sharks alone.'

'I'll come with you,' said his wife.

Albert looked curiously at his wife. She never went fishing.

'Okay,' he said. 'You can't be any worse than this lot. But if you're going to be my deckie, you'll have to learn to do things right.'

'Yes, Albert,' said his little cream puff.

Every morning for a week Albert instructed his wife. Two Fijians stood waist deep in the water alongside Albert's Blackfin. Between them was a large hessian sack filled with coconuts. They liked Albert. They liked eating. They'd never had so much fish to eat in their lives.

'I've rigged up two gaffs each side,' said Albert. 'They're all tied off. All you have to do is fit the gaff to the pole. Like this.'

He showed her.

'Now you do it.'

'Now do it twenty more times.'

'Now do it ten times with your eyes shut.'

'Oh dear. Take one home and practise.'

Albert took the gaff off her and showed her how to use it.

'One behind the head, and one behind the dorsal fin,' he said. 'Head first.'

He plunged the gaff into the sack of coconuts. The Fijians grinned foolishly. The man was clearly mad.

'In, twist, up, out,' he said. 'Now you do it.'

'In, twist, oops . . .' said his little dumpling.

'Oh dear,' said the Absolute Authority on Everything. 'You'd better stay here and practise. I'll go tend to my lures.'

For a week Albert instructed his wife. And for a week he tended to his lures. He made hydroplanes to take his lures down to two hundred metres. 'Never made hydroplanes as big as this before,' he said to his little dumpling.

He cast lead bombs to take his lures down to twenty

metres and hold them steady. 'Never made lead bombs as heavy as these before,' he said to his little pudding.

He made massive lures from his marlin kit, with skirts that would fit a small child. 'Never made lures as big as these before,' he said to his little cream puff.

He made rattlers to hang off the stern with beads as big as hens' eggs. 'Never made rattlers as big as these before,' he said to his little pumpkin. 'They'll hear us coming a mile off.'

'Yes, dear,' she said. 'I've made you a new spray jacket. Never made one as nice as this before.'

'Waterproof pockets?' asked Albert.

'Yes, dear.'

'Vent in the back?'

'Yes, dear.'

'Hood?'

'Yes, dear.'

'Very nice,' said Albert. 'My favourite colours. Orange, red, yellow and silver.'

'The most visible colours to spotter aircraft,' said his wife.

'Now you're thinking,' said Albert. 'Clever little pumpkin.'

'Been quiet around here these last few days, hasn't it?' said Brewer.

'Marvellous,' said Marvin.

'Heavenly,' said Hermann.

'Like the old days,' said the manager.

'Another gin and tonic?' asked Brewer.

'Ja,' said Hermann.

'Yup,' said Marvin.

'You bet,' said the manager.

'Bombay gin,' said Brewer. 'Best gin there is in my book. Not the other rubbish. Might be all right for you, but I only drink Bombay. If you're going to have a gin and tonic, you may as well do it right.'

They nearly fell off their stools laughing. They were the happiest they'd been for one year, seven months, two weeks and three days.

'Might even be safe to turn on the lights,' said Marvin.

'My God,' said Brewer. 'Look at the size of those lures.' The contestants and their families had all arrived at the jetty for the start of the competition.

'Big lures, big fish,' said Albert.

'They're just like your spray jacket,' said Marvin.

'And almost as big,' said Hermann facetiously.

'So they are,' said Albert. He looked again at his spray jacket as if seeing it for the first time.

'Most visible colours to a spotter aircraft,' said Albert. 'My little dumpling made it for me.'

'Very nice,' said Brewer. 'Good luck.'

'Luck,' said Albert, 'has got nothing to do with it.'

'See you at the weigh-in,' said Marvin.

'Let them go out first,' said Albert, as Hermann and Brewer stepped onto Marvin's boat.

'Of course,' said his wife. 'But why?'

'So they don't follow us,' said Albert. 'It's the only chance they have.'

'Where are we going?' asked his wife.

'Deep water,' said Albert. 'Nanuku Passage. The big sharks are down deep.

'Really,' said his wife.

'Really deep,' said Albert. 'That's where the really big tigers are.'

'How big?' asked his wife.

'Really, really big,' said Albert. 'I'm going for one thousand kilos plus.'

'One thousand kilos!'

'Plus,' said the AAE. 'You must learn to listen. Wouldn't bother with anything less. Know where they are. Know how to catch them. Catch them any time I want. But at the end of the day . . .'

'I know, they're just sharks.'

'You're learning,' said Albert.

'I wonder how the others are getting on,' said his wife.

'I don't,' said Albert, 'because I know. Up to their arses in reef sharks and bronze whalers. Babes in the woods,' he said contemptuously. 'Buckets of burley, live bait. Babes in the woods.'

'Bloody hell,' said Brewer. 'There are more sharks down here than there are in the brotherhood of used car salesmen.'

'Any big ones?' asked Marvin.

'Down deep, maybe,' said Brewer. 'Problem is, how do we get our bait down through the rat pack?'

'Go out deep,' said Marvin. 'Use less burley. Start again. This time do it right.'

'Don't you start,' said Brewer.

'Wonder how our friend is getting along,' said Hermann.

'Here's the plan,' said Albert.

'Listening,' said his wife.

'This lure without a hook. It goes down on the hydroplane to two hundred metres.'

'No hook?' said his wife.

'Of course not,' said Albert. 'We'd never get him up. Not the shark we're after. That's just to bring him up.'

'Bring him up.'

'You're learning,' said Albert. 'Now this lure is bigger. And it has no hook either. It goes down on this hydroplane to sixty-five metres.'

'Right. To bring him up,' said his wife.

'Learning, learning,' said Albert. 'These two lures are bigger still. They go down on the bombs to twenty metres. They have hooks.'

'Aha!' said his wife.

'Aha, indeed,' said Albert.

'Nothing on the top?' asked his wife.

'Only us,' said the Absolute Authority on Everything. 'And the rattlers. And we wouldn't want to go any lower than we are now. No sir! Not around here. Not in these waters. Not with these lures swimming in them. Not unless you want to give some shark a nice little dumpling for dinner.' Albert laughed uproariously. They slowed down to five knots and turned into the wind. Albert put on his harness.

'A man's a fool if he has equipment and doesn't use it.'

His little dumpling steered a steady course due east towards Naitamba Island. Albert put on his spray jacket.

'Even in the tropics you can't ignore the chill factor. Not unless you're a complete idiot.'

Albert clipped himself to his safety line.

'Better safe than sorry,' he said. 'Now, hold her steady towards Naitamba while I set the lines.'

Albert set the first line at one hundred fathoms. The second at sixty-five metres. The third and fourth at twenty metres.

'Now what?' said his wife.

'We wait,' said Albert. 'What did you think?'

Deep beneath them giant creatures stirred. Far, far beneath them, prehistoric giants felt the lures' vibrations. The big fish felt hunger. The massive tiger turned slowly towards the faint signals above him, coming closer. Cautiously *galeocerdo cuvieri* began his ascent.

'How long does this go on for?' asked his wife.

'As long as it takes,' said Albert. 'What's your hurry?'

'No hurry,' said his wife.

'You look nervous,' said Albert.

'Just anxious to get it over with,' said his wife.

'Wouldn't surprise me if we had a follow right now,' said Albert.

'Oh! What was that?' asked his wife. The stubby rod holding the deepest hydroplane jerked in its socket and snapped back, line limp.

'Bingo,' said Albert.

The giant tiger shark ripped the lure off the hydroplane. Swallowed.

'Hungry,' said his brain. The hydroplane inverted, and fled to the surface.

'One down,' said Albert. 'Or one up, depending upon your point of view.'

He winched the hydroplane back on board.

'No point wasting good gear,' he said.

Nature's most efficient sea creature continued his ascent.

'Hungry,' said his brain. His colours slowly brightened. His excitement beginning to show.

'Oh!' said Albert's wife again.

'Bingo,' said Albert. 'Two down.'

The big fish ripped the lure off the hydroplane. Swallowed.

'Hungry. Hungry. Hungry,' said his brain. His colours brightening. His anger showing. The hydroplane fled to the surface. Albert winched it in.

The panic vibrations were stronger. *Galeocerdo cuvieri* continued his ascent. Two signals.

'Hungry. Hungry. Hungry,' said his brain. But the tiger was cautious, investigating one lure before switching to the other. Then back. And back again.

'Hungry. Hungry. Hungry,' insisted his brain. 'Hungry.' He increased his tailbeat. Whoosh ... whoosh ... whoosh. Each beat of his caudal fin crushing, compacting and pushing aside thousands of litres of ocean.

'Probably just deciding which lure to strike,' said Albert.
'Yes. I can see movement. Through my Polaroids.'
'Where?' asked his little dumpling.
'There,' said Albert, leaning over the transom.
'Where?' asked his little pudding, coming to look.
'There!' said Albert, leaning further over the transom.
'Right there!' said his little cream puff. And bumped Albert over.

'Fizzzzzzz . . .' went the safety line.
'Clunk,' went the spool as the line reached the end.
'Heeeeelp,' said Albert.
'Dinner time,' said his little pumpkin.
'Hungry,' said the shark's brain.

Albert knew what to do. He'd rehearsed it often enough. He could do it with his eyes closed. Albert rolled over onto his stomach. Down below him, the big shark saw the spray jacket flash orange, flash yellow, flash silver. Albert pulled himself methodically back towards the boat. Arm over arm. Legs up out of the water reducing drag. Waterproof pockets providing extra buoyancy. The twenty metres became fifteen metres became ten metres. And still he came. Closer. Closer. No cause to panic.

'Stop the boat,' said Albert.
'The throttle,' said Albert.
'Backwards,' said Albert.
'What was that, dear?' said his little dumpling. 'I must learn to listen.' She pushed the throttle.

Forwards.

'Backwards!' screamed Albert. 'Listen!'
'Fizzzzzzz ...' said the safety line.
'Clunk,' said the spool.
'Bye,' said his wife.
Albert begun to spin. Red went his jacket. Yellow went his jacket. Orange. Silver. Albert panicked.

Up above him, the big fish felt the vibrations. Up above him he saw the flash of colours. Up above him he saw the splashes, felt the disturbance, heard the rattlers.
'Food,' his brain said.
Albert spun. Orange, red, yellow, silver, orange, red, yellow, silver, orange ...
'Food,' the tiny brain in the big fish said. The giant tiger forgot about the two lures. He began his ascent.

Albert's wife saw the giant dorsal fin. Albert saw the giant dorsal fin.
'Dinner,' she said. 'Dinner, but no pudding. No dumpling. No cream puff. No little pumpkin.' She laughed.
'Eeeeeeeyyyyyaaaaaaaaaaaaaaa!' Albert said.
'Food,' said the tiger's brain.
'Food,' insisted the tiger's brain.
'FOOD.'
'FOOD. FOOD.'
'FOODFOODFOOD!'
The giant fish ripped Albert from the safety line. Swallowed.

'Albert fell overboard,' said the late Albert's wife to the gathering at the jetty. 'A big shark ate him.'

'Good grief,' said Brewer.

'Good heavens,' said Hermann.

'Good Lord,' said Marvin.

'Good God,' said the manager.

'Good riddance,' said Albert's wife. 'Somebody had to do something about that man.'

THEATRE COMES TO WOMBAT CREEK

AMY WITTING

Theatre came to Wombat Creek in 1942. It was the idea of the Methodist minister, an enthusiastic young man determined to integrate into local society, to serve the community and to be known affectionately as the Rev. To this end he had founded (and now ran) the local dramatic society, with sometimes a little too much help from the town clerk's elder daughter Lorna.

'We're doing something worthwhile if we bring entertainment to the small outlying communities,' he said.

'But could they stage it?' asked Mary, who taught English at the Central School. This was her first appointment outside the city and she felt that she was in a small outlying community already.

'There is a hall. I hold a service there once a fortnight. I was talking to Marshall from the school and he's very keen. There is a stage. It's pretty basic, but they'll improvise. I don't know about a curtain.'

'Shakespeare managed without,' said Mary. 'Keep it simple and move the furniture around between scenes. Have somebody doing an act out front, singing or something. That works all right.'

'Is it on, then?' asked the minister.

They agreed that it was on.

The programme consisted of three one-act plays, Chekhov's 'The Proposal', then a problem play about a mercy killing, called, unsurprisingly, 'A Matter of Life and Death', then a sentimental sketch about the fated Marie Antoinette.

Mary, who had suggested the Chekhov piece, had had to defend the suggestion with energy.

'Chekhov? Isn't that aiming a little high for us?'

'Listen, Rev.' That was butter. Being a conscientious atheist, she usually called him George. 'This isn't "The Three Sisters" or "The Cherry Orchard". It's a very funny piece about a proposal of marriage between two people who can't agree on anything for two minutes, except that they both want to get married. Fights about land, fights about hunting dogs ... The people around here are Chekhov's people. He understood them and they'll understand him, you'll see.'

With that last remark she had lost ground. An audibly indrawn breath from the influential elder daughter of the town clerk warned her that she was being condemned for showing off.

She took revenge. 'If you can put on that Marie Antoinette rubbish, with its expensive costumes and its silly dialogue, you can put up with a bit of real comedy from Chekhov.'

'The station people will be coming,' said Lorna. 'I suppose we want to show them a bit of refinement.'

The Rev, who did not wish to admit that he was under the thumb of the town clerk's elder daughter, said stiffly, 'It is visually charming. That is one aspect of theatre which can't be overlooked.'

'Oh yes. Dorothy will look lovely, I agree.'

'And it's not for you to talk about the expense. Seeing that we are all arranging for our own costumes.'

It was no secret that Lorna intended that her pretty younger sister should marry to advantage. Mary had discovered from the first casting that she would never appear on the stage unless her own considerable good looks were obscured by the disguise of age.

'What about staging? What about properties?'

'Bring your own milking stool,' suggested Robert.

'We are bringing a stool for Dorothy from home. The other girls will sit on cushions around her.'

'Well, that should be satisfactory,' said the Rev, who hated discord.

'We couldn't have the shadow of the guillotine projected on a backdrop, I suppose?' asked Robert. 'That would give it some point.'

'Of course not. Don't begin to complicate matters, please Robert.'

'At least give the Chekhov a reading,' said Mary.

Chekhov survived the reading because Robert wanted to play the part of Lomov. Robert worked in the bank.

At thirty-five he knew he had outlived promotion and thought now that he should have faced the uncertainties of the stage instead of choosing the death-in-life of financial security. He bore his disappointment with resignation and some elegance, but he was sure that he owed himself the part of Lomov.

The Rev would be happy to play Chubukov. He was not as talented as Robert, but he would not disgrace him.

'And what about Natalya?'

Mary looked wistful. She had taken the part for the reading and had done it well.

'We need you for Mrs Hargreaves in "Life and Death",' said the Rev. 'Nobody else could handle it.'

'Oh, well!' Mary gave way. 'Lorna for Natalya.'

Politics were politics. It had to be Lorna.

Mary consoled herself with the malicious reflection that Lorna would hardly need to act to fit the part.

So the Rev, Robert, Mary, Lorna and Dorothy with her three attendant milkmaids came to Wombat Creek. They arrived at seven o'clock in the evening, giving themselves time to assess the staging and organise accordingly. Marshall and his helpers had done their best to create a workable stage. Wide canvas drops hung from the ceiling to create wings at each side of the small stage and a row of kerosene lanterns along its edge were ready to be lit and serve as footlights. A kerosene lamp stood behind each of the canvas wings to light the path of the actors.

The Rev looked anxious.

'There isn't any dressing-room. Where are the girls to change for the sketch?'

'They will have to change in the wings,' said Lorna.

'Do you think it is safe? It will be a fire hazard, I'm afraid.'

He was aware that he should not have given in to Lorna about the Marie Antoinette sketch. It had been a showcase for vanity, and now it was a danger to life. He was punished for weakness and folly.

'They will have to change one at a time. The rest of you can use the other entrance. It isn't a chimney lamp, after all. There's no danger so long as it isn't knocked over. We can stand it well back out of the way.'

Maintaining the dignity of the cloth, the Rev said, 'I leave it in your hands, then,' quite as if he had a choice in the matter.

'The rest of you can use the other entrance. This side will be the girls' dressing-room,' said Lorna, who appeared not to have heard him. 'And you girls go straight out to sit in one of the cars as soon as you've changed. We don't want the audience to see you in costume before the sketch.'

Dorothy and her attendant milkmaids were dismayed.

'Can't we watch "The Proposal", then?'

'Oh! All right. You can start changing after the first play. Really, all these unnecessary difficulties! It seems that someone might have foreseen the need for a dressing-room!'

Mary was surveying the body of the hall.

'All those seats! Will all those people come?'

'The beetle plague last Christmas was an absolute drawcard,' said Robert.

'Oh! I suppose we can face that sort of competition.

What are those benches at the back for? Is that the gallery? The cheap seats?'

'Those are for the aborigines.'

'Goodness me! Do they know? Or does somebody say, "You sit on a bench at the back because you're an aborigine"?'

'Those are free seats, Mary,' said the Rev. His feelings were wounded, since he had fought hard for the inclusion of the aborigines. 'I suppose a white man who couldn't afford to pay would sit there, too.'

'That is a disgraceful suggestion,' said Lorna. 'I hope I never live to see a white man sitting with the aborigines.'

The Rev did not know how to deal with this without a reference to religion, which he felt would be out of place.

'Why? Does the colour come off?'

Lorna did not condescend to answer.

Mary turned to the Rev.

'If an aborigine offered to pay, could he have a chair with a back to it?'

Lorna was forced into speech.

'They don't want to mix! They're happier with their own.'

Mary nodded. 'In the circumstances, I wouldn't want to mix either.'

The Rev put his arm around her waist, an expression of Christian love to which she thought he was too much given.

'Mary, my dear. We go forward a little at a time. Let us give a good performance tonight for all those who come, and hope that to share the enjoyment of it will be a step towards real brotherhood.'

'I hear you.' And take your hand off my waist.

But he was a genuine man, doing his best, so she gave him the benefit of the doubt and waited till he removed his hand of his own accord.

Before eight o'clock the hall was full and the benches at the back crowded with aboriginal families, all smiling, unaware that they had been insulted.

At eight precisely, Robert and the Rev stepped onto the uncurtained stage and began what became the hit of the evening. Mary was vindicated. She had been compelled by popular opinion to cut the scene and adapt some of the dialogue. Nevertheless, Chekhov rose triumphant. The audience laughed that quiet, abandoned laughter which is far from disorder and indicates complete surrender.

'How odd,' she thought. 'Coming to a little bush town to a stage with kerosene footlights and no curtain, to see something you'd be lucky to see at Covent Garden. What a pity Robert didn't take to the stage. And the Rev isn't so bad either.' Lorna as she had foreseen had hardly needed to act at all. What was it? 'Learn your lines and don't bump into the furniture. Particularly when it's kerosene lamps.'

She was so happy, so much in love with these people who appreciated Chekhov, that she could endure even the sight of Lorna, standing between Robert and the Rev, hands linked, bowing and smiling, elated by the energy of the applause.

The clapping went on and on. The three stars continued to bow. Julia Scobie, who was about to render 'I'll See You

Again', accompanied by Mrs Scobie at the piano, was growing nervous. Mary was already wearing the make-up which transformed her into the anguished, middle-aged Mrs Hargreaves, Robert had only to change his jacket and tie to make his brief appearance as the doctor, but the Rev had to have his head dressed in a series of bandages which would indicate massive brain damage and leave only his eyes and his mouth visible. Mary had practised the procedure till she was confident there would be no comic mishap with the make-up, but it still took time and in the poor lighting and narrow area of the improvised wings, confidence and a steady hand.

'Get off the stage, you silly asses,' she thought as she waited off-stage with a handful of bandages, ready to transform the Rev into the near-corpse of her injured son.

'And about time, too,' she said, laughing, as he settled into the armchair with castors which was the best substitute they had been able to find for an invalid chair.

'You are just as happy as we are,' said the Rev. 'They certainly proved you right about Chekhov.'

'You were both wonderful. Now keep quiet and hold still. Have you got your slippers? Where's the sheet?'

'I have it,' said Robert, 'and the carafe and the glass. The phial is in my pocket. Do not panic.'

'Who's panicking? I'm just not wasting time, that's all.'

She applied a bandage which immobilised the Rev's jaw, pinned it tightly at the top of his skull, and finished the work just as Julia's first song ended.

The audience responded with a deep sigh of appreciation which made them look at each other in astonishment.

'Julia is reaching them tonight,' said Robert. 'I didn't know she had so much audience appeal.'

Mary draped the sheet over the Rev, to conceal Chubukov's formal suit, checked that he had changed from shoes to slippers, and relaxed.

The clapping which followed the sigh was polite, but unemphatic.

Julia began to sing 'Blue Skies'. That was the cue for the cast to take the stage, push the armchair into position, set up their properties and then remain motionless in position till the song ended.

'Here we go,' said Robert. 'On your mark, Mrs Hargreaves!'

Mary did not like the play. At the first reading, she had muttered to Robert, 'Dead! Dead! And never called me Mother!' He had answered with a nod of understanding, but the play was the Rev's choice, against which there was no appeal. She did however enjoy playing the part and believed that she had made something of it.

The song ended, the clapping ceased and the statues came to life.

'Is there no hope, Doctor?'

'I am sorry, Mrs Hargreaves. It would be wrong to hold out any false hopes, I am afraid. The brain damage is extensive. The most we can do is relieve the pain.'

Presentation of the fatal phial.

'I must warn you to take care in administering the dose. Five drops is the maximum. Any more would be dangerous. Ten drops would mean instant death.'

'I understand, Doctor. I shall take care.'

The doctor departed. Mary picked up the phial, studied it, put it down, looked towards the armchair and began her one-sided conversation with the near-corpse.

'What goes on in your mind? Do you have memories? Happy ones? The match where you scored that field goal in the last minute? The holiday in the snow?'

'I shall consider it a triumph,' she had said to Robert, 'if I can get through this without making anyone laugh.'

But she was getting through it very well. The audience was silent, even tense.

She came to the end of happy memories. 'If only you could speak to me. If only I could know!'

The near-corpse obliged, on cue, with a groan of pain.

Mary picked up the carafe, poured a glass of water, picked up the phial and poured five drops.

The near-corpse groaned again.

'Better dead,' muttered Mary. 'Better dead.'

She picked up the fatal phial, looked towards the exit and said, 'You put a weapon in my hand, Doctor. Did you know what you were doing? Did you understand what choice you gave me?'

From the audience a voice cried out in anguish, 'Oh, my Gawd! *She's going to do him in!*'

A second of silence, then a vast roar of laughter. Problem play became farce. As Mary poured the killing dose into the glass, voices counted gleefully, 'Six! Seven! Eight!' and they cheered the fatal tenth. They were clearly advocates of euthanasia and made their opinion known without inhibition.

'No worse than 2E on a windy afternoon,' thought

Mary, going calmly on with her mime of anguish and indecision. As she approached the near-corpse and held the fatal dose to its lips, its hand rose and squeezed her free hand consolingly.

'That's right. Stage a miracle recovery. That's all we need,' she thought, sincerely angry with the Rev for his lack of stage discipline, but there was no laugh this time. The audience had become oddly quiet.

The communal mind seemed to be elsewhere. Then came that odd sigh, which surely had little to do with the question of euthanasia.

Mary as a final gesture clasped her dying son to her bosom, wishing fiercely that she could wring his bloody neck instead.

This was where one felt the lack of a curtain. Robert reappeared, they bowed to the audience, acknowledged spattered applause, pushed the armchair into the wings and drew a breath of relief.

Mrs Scobie had begun a piano piece, an Etude of Chopin's, while the Rev emerged from his bandages, saying, 'Sorry, luv.'

Robert seized Mary's wrist and dragged her away from sympathy.

'Quick! You mustn't miss this!' He led her down the steps into the hall, stopped halfway along the side aisle and pointed. 'I knew there must be something going on. I had to find out what it was. Look at that!'

Clearly defined on the canvas drop, the gigantic shadow of Dorothy, the town clerk's pretty younger daughter, was stepping out of a skirt. It was already shirtless. It bent to adjust a suspender and tighten a stocking. The audience held its breath.

'The girls' dressing-room,' said Robert. 'An alternative attraction, obviously.'

'My God! If this doesn't bring in the broad acres, nothing will!'

'Oh, you are a wicked little bitch, aren't you?' said Robert, with a giggle which made her dismiss him, regretfully, as a marriage prospect.

She giggled too.

'Do you think the aborigines are mixing? Or are they keeping their eyes shut, like good little boongs?'

'Oh, hush. You will bring society down in ruins around us.'

'Somebody should have warned them, just the same.'

'It's too late. It was too late as soon as it began. Silence will reign. You'll see.' As the figure disappeared into the milkmaid disguise of Marie Antoinette, the crowd exhaled.

Mrs Scobie at the piano was gratified. 'These people respond to beauty when it is offered to them,' she thought. 'One must have the courage to offer it, not to condescend to them.'

Something had indeed put them in the mood for Chopin. They applauded with conviction, if not with vigour.

Marie Antoinette appeared with her attendant milkmaids, sat on her stool and spoke wistfully of the joys of a simple life and the discomforts of royalty.

The girls came forward hand in hand and bowed to the audience. They must have been astonished by the great roar of appreciation which accompanied the clapping, for they had never before met with such appreciation of their acting talent. Blushing and smiling, they bowed again and again, until Mrs Scobie began to play 'God Save the King', to indicate the end of the programme.

Their innocence affected Mary more than her own disaster, which after all had been a comic affair. 'I hope they never find out,' she thought. Robert had said, after all, 'Silence will reign.' If only that was true.

The stalwarts of the Country Women's Association, who profited by the proceeds of ticket sales, entertained the cast with local notables to supper in the schoolroom. In the third year of the World War, the supper table gleamed like a dream projected by greed and deprivation: three pavlovas topped with whipped cream and passionfruit, strawberry cream sponge, lemon cheese tarts, caramel tarts, melting moments – names now part of legend to the strangers.

'How do they do it?' asked Mary, who was wondering how much she could ask of her appetite.

'You're in the country now,' said the Rev. 'It's no surprise to me. They give me afternoon tea after service on Sundays. Mind you, I think there's a little innocent bartering of sugar coupons in exchange for butter and cream.'

Robert took a sanctimonious tone. 'A small sin, Reverend, but a sin nonetheless.'

'I prefer to regard it as Christian charity,' said the Rev, smiling at the woman who was approaching with a stack of plates.

'You'll help yourselves, won't you?'

'With alacrity,' said Robert.

'They are overcome by the sight of so much glorious food,' said the Reverend.

'But we want you to come back! Such a wonderful evening! We all enjoyed it so much. If we feed you well, you might come again.'

They had approached the table, plate in hand. Others joined the conversation.

'That first piece. Didn't it put you in mind of the Wilkins? Dad always used to say it was lucky Merle and Hubert didn't have to walk up the aisle together. They wouldn't have made it to the altar without starting an argument. Merle would have been saying "I don't" instead of "I do".'

'Which might have been just as well, all things considered,' said a neighbour.

'Oh, I don't know. They got on well enough. They just liked an argument, that's all.'

'I don't think I'll be trying Mrs Hargreaves again,' said Mary, aware that nobody else would bring up the topic and determined not to let it pass in silence.

They were embarrassed.

'A little above the heads of the audience, perhaps. A bit on the serious side.'

'It might have started out serious, but it certainly didn't end that way. I thought it was a hoot,' Mary lied. 'I had trouble keeping my face straight, myself. I could hardly keep my face straight.'

'Not your fault, Mary,' said the Rev. 'You did well. A little too well, perhaps.'

'Indeed you did. But we must agree,' one of the hostesses said to Robert, 'that you were the hit of the evening.'

'But I wasn't up against much competition. I don't think I could have competed with the milkmaids. I'm quite sure that they were the hit of the evening.'

The Rev looked puzzled. Heads turned towards Robert, pairs of eyes gunned him down. Knowing that he had said all that was permissible, he smiled demurely and turned his attention once more to the slice of pavlova on his plate.

One day the shadow show on the back wall would be local legend, good for a tale and a reminiscent smile. For the present, it was under the embargo of hospitality – and, thought Mary, of kindness. The milkmaids would never know the whole of their contribution to the evening's entertainment.

They understood conduct at Wombat Creek.

VILLA ADRIANA

SHIRLEY HAZZARD

They got down from the bus in the middle of a straight, flat stretch of the Via Tiburtina. It was the midday bus from Rome, loaded with visiting relatives and returning farmers, and at the windows heads turned to watch the two foreigners descend to the country road. First, the man got down, his camera strap over his shoulder, his jacket over his arm, a book in his hand. The bus waited, quivering. He extended his free hand to the woman, who, slightly gathering her dress, negotiated the deep steps.

'*Vanno alla villa*' was exchanged around the bus.

The conductor called to the driver, the door clanged, and they were left behind in a cloud of dust.

Because this was the higher part of the plain across which they had come, they could see it stretching back in the direction of Rome – a dry, untidy shrubbery posted with olive trees and cypresses and a litter of small houses, rammed by the sun. Behind them, where the bus was already climbing the steep slope to Tivoli, the mountains were white, almost featureless in the heat, and scrabbled with vineyards and umbrella pines.

'VILLA ADRIANA,' said the notice under which they turned off into a lane. Where it joined the main road, the lane was quite suburban. It was lined with raw, shuttered houses and with groups of oleanders that gave no shade and weighted the air with a sugary smell. But a little farther the countryside closed in, and the two of them wandered on in shadow, scarcely speaking, her hand through the crook of his free arm. In the middle of a wood, the trees gave way to a parking area. Crossing this open space between two empty tourist buses, they entered the gates of the villa.

'So you see,' she said, as though they had been having a long conversation, 'there wouldn't be much point.' They rounded a corner and stopped in the avenue to look at the ruins of a small amphitheater.

'This is called the Greek Theater.' He closed his book, and they walked on between two lines of magnificent cypresses.

'I'm sure you agree,' she continued, with that offhandedness, he thought, so uncharacteristic of her, that she had developed in these last few days – like a parody of what she objected to in his own manner. As if to irritate him even further, she added, 'on the whole', as they paused at the top of the avenue before one extremity of a colossal wall.

There was a restaurant to the right, among the trees. 'Shall we have something now, or later?' he asked her.

'It's so hot,' she said.

He put his book in his pocket, and they went into the café and stood at the bar. The boy took two wet glasses from the draining board and filled them with *aranciata*. In the garden at the back, a girl was clearing the deserted lunch tables. Her stiff, short skirt spread out around her and exposed the backs of her knees each time she bent over to collect another dish. She took, in her high-heeled sandals, such tiny, tapping steps that it seemed she would never complete the journey from one table to the next. Now and then she glanced at the boy in the bar, and whenever she looked up he was watching her.

'On the whole' indeed, the man thought angrily as they left the café and passed through a gap in the great wall into an open field of ruins. 'I'm not quite sure what we're talking about,' he told her, although nothing more had been said.

'Simply that it wouldn't work.' She stood still to gaze at a sheet of water, a long, shallow pond in which a few lilies were trailing. 'We would make one another unhappy – we do already – and it's as well that we found out in time. That's all. It's quite impossible.'

'I don't understand,' he said stubbornly.

'And that,' she returned, 'is precisely why.'

I must have hurt her vanity, he decided, since she was not usually cruel. Opinionated, sulky sometimes – but even that she couldn't sustain; she would give in at the first appeal. (Preferring consistency, he could not value such concessions.) If he were to say now, for example, whatever it might be she wanted him to say – that nothing mattered to him but their love for each other, something along those lines – she would come round. Though why she should need that, why she minded so, he couldn't imagine. She herself, after all, had other things in her life, had, in fact, loved before this, more intensely; he didn't know who it was – and had not the least desire to know, he told himself, his mind ranging hastily over the circle of their friends.

'I don't really think you care deeply about anything,' she was saying now, as though the observation might be of passing interest. 'Except, of course, your work.'

He reflected that she was probably the only person he knew who didn't attach importance to his work. And it *was* important; something would be changed in the field, however imperceptibly, when his book came out. She, who knew nothing, nothing at all, and was always exalting her miserable intuitions into the sphere of knowledge – how dare she speak of his interest in his work as though it were something pedestrian, discreditable? She had no feeling for the elements, the composition of things. Once, for instance, in Rome, they had seen an ancient inscription on a wall, and he had begun to translate it aloud when she, brushing aside the syntax, rendered the sense of it in half a dozen words and turned away, having temporarily deprived him of his reason for living.

'Perhaps it's true that I care most about my work,' he said. 'But then I do care – about other things. In any case, I can't be what I'm not.'

They were walking now on a path of small stones.

She persisted, relentlessly: 'You gave a different impression when we first knew each other.'

He halted, opening his hands helplessly. 'Well – that was human.'

This, unexpectedly, seemed to be an acceptable answer, and they turned off the path into a vast shell of red Roman brick, and entered an inner courtyard. Water was seeping over the ruined paving and around the plinths of the broken columns that unevenly supported the sky. Releasing his arm, in which her own had remained, she made her way across the drier slabs of stone to a pillar and seated herself in its shadow.

He followed her, reopening his guidebook. 'This must be Hadrian's retreat – the Maritime Theater,' he said. He sat down on the base of the column, and they held the book between them.

> We love to indulge in the generally entertained tradition, and fancy the Emperor Hadrian in his moments of spleen and misanthropy slipping off by himself and recover his spirits from the grievous weight of the care of the empire ...

She took off one of her sandals and inspected a blister on her foot. Pulling the strap back over her heel, she glanced at the young man, who was reading carefully. To him, she thought, life was a series of details – a mosaic rather than, say, a painting. He had to have reasons for everything, even if it meant contorting human nature to make it fit into them; so concerned with cause, he ignored consequence. And sometimes, no doubt, it was the right thing. It was the way men's minds worked, she supposed;

the process, in fact, by which the world was provided with machines and roads and bridges – and ruins. But they chose to forget that their whole system of logic could be overturned by the gesture of a woman or a child, or by a single line of poetry. This business of reasoning, she reflected, was all very well, within reason, but if one had nothing to be passionate about one might as well be dead.

'... from the grievous weight of the care of the empire,' she read again. They were, very slightly, leaning on each other.

'*Und hier, meine Damen und Herren, war die Zufluchtstätte des Kaisers*,' said a voice behind them.

There were about a dozen in the group, all with reddened faces under their new straw hats, all with woollen socks under their new sandals, all, she noticed, with cameras and guidebooks. They assembled inside the arch, and made notes as the guide pointed and explained. '*Man nennt es das Wassertheater ...*'

The two by the column sat in silence until the group withdrew. Then she clasped her hands around her knees, turning to him. 'It's just that you do seem to take yourself rather seriously,' she said.

He considered this. 'Well ... in the end, I suppose, one must.'

'Exactly. So why begin that way?' But this she said almost as an entreaty, adding: 'Anyway, you know, you're so much better than I.'

'In what way, for God's sake?'

'Oh, I don't know. Accurate, reliable – '

'It sounds,' he remarked, 'like an advertisement for a watch.'

'*Et ici nous voyons le refuge de l'Empereur,*' a new voice announced from the entrance. '*On l'appelle le Théâtre Maritime.*'

'Shall we go?' he asked.

Outside, the heat was rising in waves from the plain. The withered countryside enclosing them again, the man and woman crossed a miniature railway that had been laid to carry masonry to and from the works of excavation and restoration. A workman with a paper cone on his head was crushing stones for a new path, using a roller improvised from the broken shaft of a column. They passed from the Large Baths into the Small Baths, and walked along the side of another pool, disturbing the sleep of two or three dusty swans. They found their way into a small museum, where she admired a Venus. ('Her sandals are the same as yours,' he said.) Behind the museum, a grooved track took them, through a farm, onto a wooded incline.

It was cooler on the slope. Wild flowers were growing beneath the trees and across the path. Walking in silence, they could hear the birds. The sounds of the plain came to them more remotely, for they were approaching the foot of the mountain; as they reached the first ridge, the white houses and shops of Tivoli could be distinguished, grouped high above the lines of olive trees.

Pausing on the ridge, they kissed – for some unknown reason, as she told herself, still clasped in his arms. She could see over his shoulder the next slope rising, and the next, the black pines lost in thicker vegetation or swept away in areas of cultivation. Her interest in the scene at that moment struck her as ludicrous, and she wondered if he, in his turn, might be studying the countryside behind her head. She drew back, but he kept her hand tightly in his, although the path was too narrow for them both. They were standing quite still, side by side. They might almost, she thought, have been defending one another from two different people.

'We must go back,' he said.

There was a washroom near the café, and she combed her hair in front of a scrap of mirror and attended to the sunburn on her face while he selected a table in the garden. An elderly woman in a floral apron brought her a can of cold water, and she washed her feet, sitting on a white wooden chair borrowed from the restaurant. When she took off her sandals, the woman carried them out and brushed them in the garden, and stood watching her while she put them on again.

'Your husband?' the woman asked, smiling and nodding toward the restaurant.

'Yes,' she said, because it seemed simpler.

They had a table in the shade. The waitress, moving slowly across the garden, arrived at last beside them and set down their drinks on the cloth. There was a different boy in the bar.

'When I ordered,' the man said, 'she asked me if we were married.'

'What did you tell her?'

He looked surprised. 'Why – that we weren't, naturally.'

Even under the trees, the heat was intense. She lifted her hands from the table and closed them around the cold glass.

'There's a bus in half an hour,' he said. 'We should just do it. We may even see it coming down from Tivoli.' He thought she seemed tired, but then they had been walking all afternoon. And they hadn't decided anything – although at one point, he remembered, she had told him that it was impossible. She was looking at him, and for a moment he thought he would be able to tell her that nothing else mattered (or whatever it was). But they had walked too far; his head ached slightly from the sun. And now she had turned aside.

EILEEN'S CHRISTMAS FUDGE

GILLIAN MEARS

On the drive to Eileen's house in Bessie Street, a morning storm precedes me, clearing a swathe through the jacaranda flowers on the road and pulling them into the air. It is as if an invisible king, shaking his head, has suddenly seized his purple robe and flown away with the west wind. Fanciful, I think, shaking my own head. I am always prone to the fanciful on the drive to see Eileen Challacombe who at 81 is my oldest friend. Some flowers race ahead of my car and are lost in the edges of grass so that although it's only October and Eileen still apparently invincible, I feel a terrible pang rising in my throat which threatens to swallow the morning we have planned. Old friends cannot last forever, the airborne cape of flowers seems to be saying. Everything is impermanent, even Eileen.

I'm on my way to Eileen's not to massage her feet as is usual but to learn the secret art of the chocolate fudge she's been making for my family for at least a quarter of a century. The fudge, packed always in an old biscuit tin, with a small tag full of her indecipherable script, has arrived without fail for all the Christmases I've ever had at home in Grafton.

Eileen's fudge once travelled airmail to France via a thoughtful young sister, who unable to imagine my Christmas without such sweetness, packed 4 fat squares. I ate the fudge in snow near the Geneva border and it brought with it memories of the uproarious way Eileen and my mother would laugh together in hot Januarys in Grafton. Brushing snow off my face, I looked through a low window to see a friend, dancing for her mother. My friend was wearing only her bra and pants and from the mother's wrist dangled a small camera. When they realised I'd seen them, they looked so abashed and grave, that in my guilt I bolted down the remaining two pieces of fudge without attending properly to its qualities. Chocolate fudge. Never any other flavour. It would seem wrong to tamper with the recipe which Eileen wrote out for me a year ago but which, many batches of chocolate sludge and chocolate crumbs later, I've totally failed to perfect. Months have gone by, the whole year, as if shot by the indifferent catapult of some old God.

'It's a bit pale,' Eileen says dubiously, looking at the poor attempt I've brought to show her today. And indeed as we peer into the tin the fudge under our gaze looks like it has hepatitis. 'And thin. Bloody hell! What on earth have you done to it?!'

I mumble something about the electric beater.

'Well, no wonder! An electric beater.'

Always there is something king-like about Eileen, even when she's swearing. At 81 she is neither particularly male or female but simply regal. In her purple cardigan lined with even deeper purple silk, she leads me imperiously through to her small kitchen. I hear her wheezing, each breath so deep and considered it's as if these ten steps are the final ones of a gruelling marathon.

'Yes,' says Eileen, waving an old square aluminium pan. 'I would've used this for every batch of fudge I ever made the Mears. You see! All those scratches and holes are where I've cut it with a knife.' The pan is ancient with a yellow, shiny patina. 'I've never used another tin. I suppose it is kind of magic. And I never wash it. Just a rinse and you'd never know.'

Until today I have always imagined Eileen at Christmas time toiling over huge cauldrons of fudge for her numerous friends and their families but it hasn't been like that at all. Oh no, she says, she does not distribute her fudge to just everyone. Apart from the batch she makes for her own family at Christmas, my family and the Anglican Cathedral's dean are the only other blessed recipients. I think of the good fortune of the Mears family to have known Eileen and of how short the time is left to bestow our gratitude and love.

As Eileen begins to measure the milk and sugar into an equally battered saucepan, I look outside the kitchen window. Honeysuckle is pouring over the abandoned chicken run in more fervent flower than ever before. When I first came to this house as a ten year old, Dick her husband was dying of lung cancer. There was the smell of flowers then too as he sat under a rug and offered me peppermints.

'Never double the recipe,' Eileen is saying. 'Cows' milk is the best. You know. Real. But we can't have that today. White sugar. I'm not sure what would happen with raw sugar. I don't know. It's just one of those things, I don't know. If I do have a failure it's because of the weather.'

For years after Dick's death, throughout my childhood, I'd scribble Eileen mad little notes, imploring her to stop smoking but it's only in the last few years that her own lungs and airways have forced the issue. By the dining table, so long and deep and afloat with the petals of flowering orchids, stands the oxygen tank. It is ugly and grey, like an old astronaut's relic. Eileen, on the other hand, banging a sifter full of chocolate drinking powder into the saucepan because she says it's inclined to go a bit knobby, seems alive beyond belief. Saying that she goes by colour alone, she taps in a bit more powder.

The little dark loyal cocker spaniel leaps around and around as if to emphasise the lightning speed of the past; the little spaniel Eileen says might have to be put to sleep upon Eileen's death for Eileen's fear is that the dog will not bond with anyone else. She has slept with Eileen since puppyhood and given birth to puppies of her own on Eileen's pillows. I bend down to stroke the dog's ears which are smooth and rich with a texture of velvet curtains.

The milk, says Eileen, is taking longer to boil in the stormy weather. As the alchemical mixture thickens against the wooden spoon, so do our memories. Eileen is remembering her boys when they were little, Peter and Jeremy, and how the fudge, which she never limited, would be demolished. And how it is the same now with the already grown up grandchildren.

I am thinking of Peter when he was the chef at the Loaded Dog, before he grew sick and died – his exquisite abilities with chocolate and eggs. How upset he was when a husband I was with ate two chocolate mousses without a hint of mindfulness.

'It was Peter's birthday you know, the other day,' says Eileen, 'And when I went out to the grave, someone had been there, obviously at night, sitting there with him with a candle.'

We bow our heads at the memory of Peter, speculating which friend, which lover, lit the candle and sadly I stroke a leaf of his bonsai fig on the kitchen counter which has grown luxurious beyond belief in his long absence. I'm thinking of how in the eating of sugar we are really encountering the never-ending search for love. And how transient, I think, how brief a burst of life to be buried before forty Christmases have passed. How can it sometimes be borne?

'This is how you do it,' says Eileen from her stool, her hand moving clockwise and lopsided, in and out of the sweet steam, and shaking away the mood with a recollection of other confectioneries of the past. 'Divinity Creams! You didn't have them smooth. You lay them in little blobs all around, you know, and they were superb. My mother taught me. This is her fudge recipe from England. I don't ever remember it in China. When the new Dean came I thought blow it, I won't do the fudge anymore, but then I read in the paper that he loves chocolate. Last Christmas

EILEEN'S CHRISTMAS FUDGE

I had such a lovely letter. It's sad. I can't eat chocolate really anymore. I get these little mouth ulcers. The cortisone.

'It's coming along now. Fetch out the jug of cold water from the fridge. Let's see if it will make a bit of a ball.'

For a moment we fall silent and there is just the deep bubble of the fudge on the stove interspersed with noises of the galahs outside and of us taking turns to eat the small blobs of fudge hardening in the water. 'This is an old, old spoon,' she thinks to say, lifting it out to drop another drip of mixture into the water. 'A mouse has chewed it but it doesn't matter. It's the balance,' she says, showing me its long wooden handle. 'Over there's a modern spoon and I never use it. Or very, very rarely.'

With the pan off the heat and one walnut of butter dropped in, Eileen switches to a stool by the sink and begins the final transformation. 'Now you just sit and stir. You see? This is a nice placid job. Just gently. My mother would do everything gently, she was such a weak stupid little thing. But she would have at least four glasses of cold water all in a row. I'd have everything out for her. We'd make lots for Christmas parties. I can remember making it most of all in Maidenhead, Berkshire, the house on the Thames. We had a boathouse with boats we had to work on. You know, row or paddle. A punt.' For a moment the wooden spoon becomes a pole gliding through the river. The morning seems to slow right down as if mesmerised like myself by the muffled tock of the wooden spoon against the saucepan. 'My arm's getting tired now,' she says. 'I think I've got to pour it. Risk it. Here's the pan.'

Now Eileen's breathing worsens as if involved in the

most strenuous labour of all and I want to beg her please to have some oxygen. But pools of light have gathered on the surface of the fudge and she leans over the reflections like a beautiful Chinese crane in old silk thread. 'It may not even work you know today,' she says and one hand goes down to stroke her spaniel's ears and to offer the dog a little of the fudge hardening already on the edges. I tell her how the youngest Mears child, who ate so much of her tin of fudge last year he swears he'll be more cautious this Christmas coming, has even called his small black and white terrier Fudge.

'Here, try some,' says Eileen so that I remember all over again its addictive nature. 'God, I hope it's going to work.'

'It is tender, Eileen,' I say.

She gives her secret smile and says that it seems it isn't going to be a bad batch. 'I always mean to time myself. I forget. I will one day. My cutting's never been very good though. This is where my shaky hand comes in.'

Well, I try to explain, the wonder of this is that the lucky recipients of a fudge tin can then choose large or small pieces or even crumbs if their consumption has been excessive. I want to say how the fudge hits the tongue so intensely it might as well still be boiling.

But dramatically and with no warning, Eileen has upended the fudge onto the counter. 'I'm pushing it a bit,' she says dramatically but holding up a square by its soft wet edges it is quite clearly a triumph. I can see sugar crystals, the sun shining through. And the moment Eileen turns her back, the little dog adeptly with her front paws up, scooping a square into her mouth.

When I leave it is with the instructions to go via the Cathedral. On the off chance the Dean is wandering about, I am to offer some fudge, resplendent in its tin, as a kind of early emissary to Christmas. But although there is a wet umbrella leaning against the cathedral wall I can see no one. As if in a temple in Asia, and the better to walk, I take off my shoes. At first I stand for a while before Peter's stained glass memorial window. This depicts St Michael slaying the dragon, the palm tree outside so appropriately like a tall exotic dancer in a grass skirt at the Albury Hotel. Then noiselessly I go into the fluted ceiling of the baptistery. Here are the smaller, pointier memorial windows of Dick and Eileen. The colours are acute, the dress of Mary holding the baby see-through and sea blue. I turn around to the marble angel and the font and smile to see that a Pyrex bowl, that could be used in the making of confectionery, rests beneath the angel for blessing the heads and hearts of the new babies. The stained glass Jesus is so swaddled he looks like a butterfly cocoon about to hatch but his face is wizened.

Because I can't find the Dean I take out a piece of fudge and in the Baptistery, sitting on the long pew next to the teacups, nibble slowly. A year or so ago, the fudge makes me remember, I was late home for Christmas and came into a house full of sleeping children. I found a likely looking tin, yes, tagged with Eileen's own inimitable messages for Christmas. Ahh, I thought. After the long drive, some real sweetness and a cup of tea but in the light of the fridge I realised that the tin was quite empty, even of crumbs.

In the Cathedral I look out and along to the aisle where Eileen always sits. Second pew row, second seat along and to where one day I will look only to the memory of Eileen.

As is the way of Eileen's fudge, you can never stop at one piece. So another square, a little larger than the first and finally one third bit. I put the fudge into my mouth as a kind of communion with the past and future and with a small sticky prayer of thanks to its maker leave the Cathedral, the tin of fudge heavy in my hands.

TEA AND BISCUITS
WITH RICHIE BENAUD

CHRIS DAFFEY

Matthew Bradbury was from the old school of Phys. Ed. teachers. As such, he lived his life according to three simple maxims:

(a) sport is good;
(b) it's never too cold to wear shorts; and
(c) there's nothing on this earth you can't accomplish with a cleft chin, a pair of dark-blue Stubbies and a can of Old Spice.

With his rugged physique, chiselled features and unhealthy obsession with blowing whistles, Matthew could be described as the perfect embodiment of the old-school ethos. He was fit, he was impervious to all weather conditions, and he ate more fibre in a week than most people consume in a lifetime.

In line with his no-nonsense outlook on life, Matthew

had an equally straightforward approach to education. According to the Bradbury Big Book of Clever, there was no question too difficult, no dilemma too complex, that it couldn't be solved through a liberal application of common sense and a brisk jog around the block. So confident was Matt Bradbury in the power of his homespun logic that he frequently strayed outside the role of PE instructor and expressed opinions on a whole range of subjects, such as:

- Science and Technology ('Atoms are like tiny, tiny tennis balls, but smaller and more explosive');
- the Arts ('Has anyone in this class seen *Caddyshack*?'); and
- Sex Education ('Okay, boys, watch my hands move. You have one of these, they have one of those – BANG – there you have it. Any questions?').

Yep, it was a pretty black and white world out there for Matt Bradbury. And in that world there were only two types of cricketers – 'those who could play' and 'uncos'. On a scorching March afternoon, I fronted up to the school oval in the hope of distancing myself from the latter category.

Like many primary school sportsgrounds, the school 'oval' was actually more of a rectangle than anything else. People just referred to it as an oval because it sounded stupid to say 'let's have a kick of the footy on the oblong'. To a twelve-year-old eye, the oval looked massive. Its loosely sown turf and countless sprinkler caps stretched nearly sixty metres from the St Marks church fence to the sloping embankment separating the ground from the rest of the school. It was an awesome arena by primary school standards and the perfect venue for the epic struggle that was about to unfold. Thirty-six combatants strode onto the field that day, and only fifteen would walk off with a coveted place in the Templestowe Heights First Eleven. All my plans for my grade six year hinged on me being one of them.

Making the First Eleven was as impossible as it was desirable. To get in, you had to be good at cricket. I was shit at cricket. Well, shit's an exaggeration. I was stock-standard average – a talentless but gritty toiler who'd built a solid reputation in the backyard form of the game, but failed to make the jump to flat pitches and hard balls. With short boundaries, furry tennis balls and my sister bowling offspin, I was unstoppable. With long boundaries, polished Kookaburras and males my own age, I was bloody awful. I had more chance of sneezing bullion than I did of making the school cricket team, but I was determined to try anyway.

The rewards you received for making the First Eleven made even the most futile attempts to get into it seem worthwhile. Membership of the side was like a gold pass to social acceptability. For those lucky enough to be selected in the squad each year, life was an endless parade of backslapping well-wishers, attractive girlfriends and fashionable parties (the kind with brand-name soft drinks and no games involving donkeys). The First Eleven was much less about sport than it was about status, and the list of certainties for this year's team read like a Who's Who of the playground elite. Amongst those almost guaranteed a spot were:

- Scott Brenner (a talented opening batsman and all-round nice guy who was expected to captain the side);
- Alex Milano (a flashy left-hander whose immaculate cover drive and ability to lay foot-long bogs were the stuff of legend);
- Marty Goldbloom (a terrifying fast paceman who could knock the head off an ox from twenty paces);
- and last, but by no means least, Jeremy Ng (whose lightning reflexes and wizardry behind the stumps more than compensated for a loose grasp of English and an unpronounceable surname).

These were the kids who oozed the Right Stuff. These were the guys who held the playground in the palms of their hands. They were Templestowe Heights' finest, and if I'd ever had the opportunity, I'd have tied them all together, dropped them in an enormous tub of gelignite, and blown them all to bits. All of them. Even the nice ones.

Mr Bradbury kicked off proceedings with a brief outline of the rules. It was standard trials format. Everyone was divided up into pairs, and each pair got to bat and bowl for two overs. Once this had been explained to us in excruciating detail, Mr Bradbury clapped his hands together, blew his whistle a couple of times, and then signalled for the group to disperse. The trials had begun.

Having won the toss, my team filed off the ground and settled itself down on the embankment. Our opposition went into the field. Much to the relief of myself and the other cricketing minnows present that day, the division of the group into two teams had been attended to personally by Mr Bradbury (who'd posted up lists on the canteen noticeboard the day before). The alternative would have been to appoint two captains and let them pick the sides, player by player. That alternative was horrifying.

There are few times in life where your relative merit as a person is so brutally and publicly adjudged as when you stand before two captains waiting to be deemed worthy of their team. They look at you, they assess you, they weigh your strengths and weaknesses against those of your peers, and then slowly and methodically, they rank you:

> 'Mark, you're the best; Andy, you're second; Tim, Matt and Trent, you guys fit in the middle somewhere; Paulo, Max and that fat kid with his finger in his ear, you're all pretty shit . . .'

And so on and so forth, until thirty people are crowded around the two gangliest, least coordinated kids in the group, trying to decide which one is more tolerable than the other. After what seems like an eternity of last-minute deliberations, a decision is finally made. Slightly less awful Ross peels off to one side, leaving the truly, despicably awful Gavin to trudge off to a team that never expressed even the slightest preference in his favour. The verdict is in, the people have spoken –

'Gavin, you are quite simply the absolute worst. And

there's no one in the entire school we'd less like to have aboard than you.'

It was cruel, it was barbaric and it undoubtedly destroyed lives. But it produced fair teams, and that was what was important.

As luck would have it, my team happened to include my best friend, Martin Timms. Martin actually had a legitimate chance of making the side. He was a solid left-handed batsman, a handy medium pacer and was renowned for having a great 'cricket brain' (whatever the hell that meant). As we sat on the grass fiddling with our equipment, he attempted to impart some of his cricketing wisdom –

'Now don't forget what I showed you, Daff. Keep your eye on the ball, take each delivery on its merits, and for God's sake play straight!'

I nodded my head respectfully.

'Oh, and another thing,' he added, as I stuffed a worn, plastic box down my pants. 'If you get hit in the goolies, don't let the opposition see your pain. Don't give 'em the satisfaction, Daffa. Don't give 'em the satisfaction.'

He was trying to be helpful, bless him. But all this talk of 'goolies' sent a shiver up my spine.

While we sat waiting for play to commence, I scanned the lunchtime crowd for Jenny's face. From what I knew of her, she wasn't a massive sports fan, so I didn't expect to see her amongst the interested onlookers gathered by the side of the oval. Sure enough, the embankment was blissfully free of striking, olive-skinned brunettes. That is, unless you counted Mario Giannopolous (which I didn't).

This was a massive relief. The last thing I needed was my prospective girlfriend thumbing her nose at me from the stands. Her absence from the crowd meant I was under a little less pressure. Unless my failure to make the First Eleven was so spectacular that it became newsworthy, she'd never hear about it. On the other hand, if Lady Luck smiled upon me (and maybe slipped me a long, brown envelope marked 'skills') and I made the team, she'd definitely hear about it. Mainly because I'd tell her. Yep, it was a win–win situation for Christopher Daffey, or at least a win–draw. And there was nothing like a risk-free, foregone conclusion to bring out my fighting spirit.

As expected, the opposition opened the bowling with Marty Goldbloom. My team responded by sending out a pair of perennial cricketing bunnies to face the music. The matching of hopelessly incompetent batsmen to murderous paceman and vice versa was standard practice in these matches. There was an automatic 'understanding' between captains that the batting side would arrange their batsmen in ascending order of competence, while the bowling side would do the opposite. It was a form of tacit collusion between the good players and was designed to eliminate the chance of one of them having a bad day and missing the team. You only had to glance at the ungainly duo clomping their way towards the pitch to realise how effective this system was.

Peter Pentagast looked like he'd last eaten a solid meal in 1974. He was five feet tall, built like a biro, and appeared to have barely enough energy to power his internal organs, let alone fend off a cricket ball. As appalling a sight as Pentagast was, though, you'd still happily hand him the strike in preference to the doofus walking out with him. Simon Jackson was a *woeful* sportsman. He wasn't fit, he wasn't fast, he wasn't strong, and he had no hand–eye co-ordination whatsoever. Combine these attributes with an unshakable belief in his own abilities and you had a fairly fatal combination. Simon Jackson stank, and everyone knew it but him.

Pentagast opted to face the first delivery of the day. It was a bold move. Rumour had it that Marty Goldbloom was expelled from his last school and almost jailed for killing a kid with a bean-ball. Apparently, one of the terms of his bond was that he had to restrict himself to medium pace or face imprisonment. Staring down the pitch at a convicted felon must have been a hard thing for Peter Pentagast. But if he was feeling the heat, he was showing no signs of it. As Marty began his long run from the canteen end, Peter calmly took guard and rolled his shoulders, like an in-form player with all the time in the world. If nothing more had happened, if all I'd seen that day was Peter's relaxed demeanour and casual stance, I would have been forced to conclude that he was a class batsman. This, presumably, was his plan. Think the goods, look the goods and maybe you'll *be* the goods. Peter was not the goods.

To say that Peter was beaten by the pace of Marty's first delivery would be a gross distortion of the facts. As far as I could tell, he didn't even realise the ball had left Marty's hand until five minutes after it'd bounced off his face. To his credit, he maintained his defiant, professional stance until the very end. Even as the shiny red cherry exploded off the pitch and thundered towards his forehead, there was no movement at all in the Pentagast camp. He just stood there and continued looking like a batsman. When he still hadn't moved a muscle three minutes after impact, Mr Bradbury and most of the players rushed to his aid. There was a brief, ill-informed discussion about whether someone could be dead standing up (Mr Bradbury in favour, most of the kids against) and then Peter was carried from the field, stance intact. It was a strange dismissal, but it was the way he would have wanted to go.

Watching Peter's lifeless carcass make its way across the ground didn't do heaps for my confidence. Simon Jackson, on the other hand, seemed to revel in it. As Marty paced out his run and Mr Bradbury cautioned him about any further short stuff, Simon jogged cheerfully up and down and practised wild hook shots. Simon too, it seemed, was determined to go down looking like a cricketer, even if he couldn't play like one. The similarity between Simon's game plan and Peter's ended there. Whereas Peter had been content with mimicking a batsman at rest, Simon wanted to show the world he could play some shots. When Mr Bradbury directed Simon to face up to the next ball, rather than the new batsman, he was rapt. He'd waited twelve long years for a chance at glory, and in his hopelessly optimistic mind, this was it.

The first time Simon was bowled, he really did look shocked. He shouldn't have been, but he was. The ball wasn't even a good one by Marty's standards, but it was more than sufficient to knock over a batsman playing a square cut to a dead straight yorker. Despite this setback, Simon was determined not to let Marty's accuracy deter him from playing his natural game. During the next over and a half, he played every shot in the book. He drove, he swept, he pulled, he hooked, and he never once got his bat near anything.

By the time Marty had finished his over, Simon's campaign was in disarray. He'd been caught once, bowled three times and stumped by the impossibly nimble Ng. At first, he tried to keep up the charade of a good batsman out of form. Each time the ball got past him, he'd spin around and stare at the shattered wicket in utter disbelief – as if it was the first time a delivery had slipped through his defences in years. Then he'd walk a few steps down the pitch, prod it with his bat and scratch his chin thoughtfully while contemplating nothing. But as time went by and more balls found their way into the woodwork, this ruse became progressively more implausible. On the third occasion that his stumps were broken, Simon merely sucked his lips together, raised his eyebrows slightly and mouthed something that looked like 'yep'.

At the end of the first two overs, our team had three runs on the board at a cost of eight wickets and one life – and the opening bowlers had booked themselves a spot in the First Eleven. It was a great result for the status quo. As expected, the next few batsmen offered a little more resistance, and slowly but surely things began to level out. I was sent in just as the battle became evenly poised.

Naturally, I was nervous. Cricket balls are hard, unyielding things, and the prospect of having one lodged in my larynx did not sit well with me. Fortunately, I had a plan. Although Martin had stressed the importance of playing each ball on its merits, I'd made up my mind to do the exact opposite. You see, a player like Martin could *afford* to play a 'wait and see' game. If the ball was good, he'd play it defensively. If the ball was bad, he'd rock back onto his back foot and club it to the fence. He was able to do this because he had a good eye and quick reflexes. The same, however, could not be said for me. By the time *I* waited to see what a ball was doing, it was always doing something bad – like hitting me in the kidneys or crashing into the stumps. No, for me, batting had nothing to do with skills or quick reflexes. It was all about anticipation. The key was to guess what the bowler was going to do, and then play your shot accordingly. If you guessed right, you looked like a champion. If you guessed wrong, you looked like a complete berk. It was an all-or-nothing strategy, but I figured it was the only chance I had.

As I commenced my long journey out into the middle, my mind began to race with the exciting possibilities a triumph might bring. I always did this. Whenever I got a sniff of success at anything I'd extrapolate it in my mind until it was out of all sensible proportion. On this particular occasion, it began with the newspapers – wonderful, spinning newspapers with huge headlines, like the kinds you see in films such as *The Bad News Bears* – 'Bears win first for season', 'Bears make it three in a row', 'Bears into playoffs', 'Bears win World Series', 'Where will it all end for those goddamned Bears?!?' Replace the word 'Bears' with 'Daffey' and ditch the baseball angle, and you've got a fair idea of the type of crap running through my mind –

'Daffey makes team!'
'Daffey shines in inter-school showdown!'
'Daffey freak selection in state squad!'
'Daffey who? Daffey how!'
'Daffey humbles England!'
'Daffey, best ever – Benaud.'

And so on and so forth, until I'm sitting next to the cream-suited one downing tea and biscuits and chatting about how I did it all for the love of the game.

It was a beautiful dream and I could've stayed in it forever. But as quickly as it came to me, it was abruptly torn away. All of a sudden the bowler was striding his way to the pitch, and reality was urgently jabbing me in the ribs.

My opponent was a kid called Steve Cohen. Steve was a good bowler, but he wasn't a great one. He was one of those players who look impressive enough in the run up (all flailing arms, puffing cheeks and lengthy strides), but who fail to transfer any of that momentum into the ball itself. For a fast runner, he was an amazingly slow bowler. As he rolled his arm over and performed some rudimentary stretches, I fiddled with my gloves and tried to guess what he was going to do. What I came up with was this –

- he knew I wasn't much of a batsman, so he'd use his first few balls to try and get me out;
- if that didn't work, he'd get pissed off and try and hit me in the head; and

- if even that failed, he'd be forced to pitch up his final ball in the hope of taking a wicket.

This was where I'd pounce.

Having worked out my plan of attack, it was just a matter of playing the appropriate shots –

Block, block, block, duck, duck, *DRIVE!*

And that's exactly what I did. I stonewalled Cohen's first three, got out of the way of the next two, and then prepared myself for one final, show-stopping slog. Everything depended on getting the right ball. If it was too full, he'd bowl me. If it was too short, he'd hit me. I needed something that was 'just so'. As Cohen thundered towards me, I shut my eyes, drew back my bat and prayed to God that it would be just short of a length. It was. I heard the ball crash into the pitch, felt it connect crisply with my bat, and then opened my eyes in time to see it spanked unceremoniously over the St Marks church fence. It was the ultimate victory of arse over skill.

'I told you it'd work!' Martin yelled, as I made my triumphant return to the embankment.

'You waited, you watched, and you kept your eye on the ball! Well done, Daff! Well done!'

I raised my bat appreciatively and thanked him for his advice. Why let the truth get in the way of a great innings?

It wasn't until I'd settled back down on the grass and removed my pads that I realised the enormity of what had just happened. I was a chance. I was actually a chance. I'd faced six balls, none of them had humiliated me, and there was now a remote possibility of scraping into the squad. Of course, I still had to bowl, but maybe I'd get lucky there too. Maybe I'd manage a couple of flukey inswingers or unplayable grubbers and then it'd all be over. Maybe, just maybe, I was actually, really, truly destined to be a member of the First Eleven. And then Jenny would just *have* to like me.

THE WASTELAND

FRANK DALBY DAVISON

Lot 32, comprising 438 acres – and known among us as de Burgh's block – had been forfeited and was available for reselection. On the advice of the Crown lands ranger, who knew his job better than the surveyor had known his, the department was permitting men who had selected in the vicinity to apply for it as an additional area. There were four of us competing for it; I, Tom Howells, who was my nearest neighbour on the southern side, Paddy McGuire who lived across the ridge on Store Creek, and a man unknown to us, not a resident of the district.

Lot 32 lay between my place and Howells', a triangular area, separating our corner-posts by a little less than a mile along the road frontage, and coming to a point where our fences met half-way along our side boundaries. It was an almost useless piece of land, mostly ridgy and barren, with its few fertile patches scattered and varying in character. In a semi-arid region such as ours, where it required ten or twelve acres of good land, well-improved, to carry a beast, its area was insufficient even had it been good. We had wondered what sort of a man de Burgh, its original selector, could be to have chosen such a block.

For a long time he kept us mystified. Up to a time when most of the settlers had been in occupation of their selections for about two years, he had not put in an appearance; nor had he responded to the written demands of Howells and myself to pay half the cost of erecting the boundary fences. Beyond his address in Brisbane, which we obtained from Wilgatown lands office, we could learn nothing of him. No one – not even the Crown lands ranger – could recall having seen him in that period when intending settlers were roaming the bush with land maps sticking out of their pockets.

In his absence – and in view of his indebtedness to me – I had entered into occupation of his property. Howells had the temporary use of the government reserve on the far side of his selection, so, by friendly agreement – arrived at with a facetious grin – he allowed me sole use and enjoyment of de Burgh's block.

I turned out on it half a dozen yearling heifers and a worn-out old horse that the surveyors had left behind. That was about the limit of its carrying capacity.

By the time de Burgh came along I had become so used to being in effective occupation that, far from being ready to offer sincere welcome to a new neighbour and fellow-pioneer, I was prepared to withdraw behind my own fences only in unavoidable recognition of his legal rights. From a condition of mind – belonging to the time when I first boiled the billy on my own fertile acres – in which I regarded de Burgh's block as one of the Creator's obvious blunders, I had come to have a high regard for it.

Down on the good lands the bush was wasting before our attack. The early days, when a man could ride from camp to camp, across country, passed with the putting up of settlers' fences. Then came ringbarking. The leaves that had filled a valley or clothed a hill fell, disclosing in their place only a mist of grey twigs supported on bare, peeling branches.

The game, too, disappeared. Mobs of kangaroos that had taken a three-point stance, with twitching nostrils, to stare at us when first we came, had vanished. The settlers' guns and the settlers' dogs had seen to that. The emu and plain-turkey were gone; and the creatures that browsed among the foliage, the koalas that glided so cleverly from view at our approach, and the possums that had peered with twinkling eyes at our camp-fires – I often wondered what tragedy had been theirs when the ringbarkers caused that cataclysm, the falling of the leaves.

Only a very impractical man would have attempted to make improvements on de Burgh's block – and even then he would have mutilated it without benefit to himself, unless there be benefit to a man in struggle, defeat, and ultimately the abandonment of hope. Yet, notwithstanding its lack of productivity, either actual or potential, it was pleasant country.

If you entered it by the sliprails in my side fence you found yourself on a narrow ribbon of grassy flat beside the creek, thinly timbered with box-trees and an occasional drooping myall. Here, in the dry end of autumn, when the budgerigars were migrating northwards, your horse's hooves rustling through the grass, would often flush them in flocks of hundreds. They would rise with a loud whirr in twittering flight, pass through the lower air like a great swirl of yellow-green gems, then swoop down and vanish into the grass again.

Across the creek you ascended a rounded hill covering a hundred acres or more. The greater part of it was clothed only with stunted brigalow; shrubs, head-high to a horseman, with light brown stems and foliage dense from the ground up, leathery in texture, sage green in colour, and looked at in the mass a billow of silvery green. It was quiet among that company of little trees. You might, if your eyes were quick, catch a glimpse of grey fur as a wallaby or a paddymelon hopped silently from your path to fresh cover. But the red iron-hard soil was barren. It was good for nothing – except stunted brigalow!

Going down the southern slope you went through a little forest of brigalow of another kind. Riding through it was like passing under a multitude of open umbrellas, edge to edge and supported from the ground on handles, black, crooked, ridiculously tall, and about as thick as a man's wrist. There was not a leaf of undergrowth and no ground life; just the forest of spindling stems, the bare earth, a little sunlight leaking between the branches and an occasional twitter of birds among the leaves.

Passing through this quaint arcade you rode them into an open-air conservatory; a forest growth of tall belah and brigalow with sunshine filtering and splashing down through leaf and soughing needle. Bottle-trees grew here – baobabs – stone-grey and squat, like monuments of primitive antiquity. Your horse trod noiselessly on ground soft with leaf-mould. In places creeping saltbush grew knee-deep, lush as lucerne, or dry and fallen back to the earth in a veined pattern of bright yellow haulm, according to the season. In the middle air sprays of foliage were held aloft on slender swaying stems.

Where clumps of prickly wait-a-while gave back the light from millions of small shiny leaves the scrub turkey had her home, her nesting mounds of leaf and forest debris. Disturbed, she would run between the bushes, or, losing faith in her legs, fly up to the topmost branches. The ground was plaited between the bushes with wallaby and paddymelon tracks. Cattle pads were plentiful, too, showing where the stock had come in from the open country to this place of shade and coolness to eat the saltbush – when dry – or to browse on the tender shoots of the shrubs. The air was sweet with the smell of greenwood and moist earth.

The settlers were felling scrub of this kind; burning it off and sowing the ashes to rhodes-grass. They were making fine grass paddocks, but of the scrub that gave way to pasture all that remained was a scattering of charred logs and blackened stumps. There wasn't enough good scrub on de Burgh's block to be worth the trouble of felling.

Following Tom Howells' fence along, you came again to open country and the creek. On the way you might cross the pad of a dingo, or even see one keeping pace with you, stopping to watch you, then gliding out of sight among the undergrowth to reappear a little later at another place;

a handsome fellow, pale biscuit-coloured, cautious, bold, secretive, curious, making you feel an intruder in the land of your birth – and then vanishing.

The waterhole was fifty yards below Tom's fence; a little pothole in the clay bed of the creek, small, but tight as a teacup, with a lofty carbeen-gum standing sentry beside it on one bank and an apple-box stretching shady green arms on the other. The cliffy banks were cut into deeply by sloping pads where the wallabies – untold generations of them – had come down at night, after making sure that brother dingo was not in hiding near by, to drink from the edge of starry waters.

Beyond the creek rose a high bony ridge, one slope covered with a pleasant but quite valueless forest of slender belahs – like ship masts – undergrowthed with wilga, waist-high. The ground life was thick; wallabies flip-flopped out of your way as you rode.

The other side was open forest, gum-topped box – a sure sign of worthless land – with scrolls of bark hanging from limb and trunk, growing on a toilsome slope where brown rocks, some as big as a dray, others as large as the end of a house, jutted from the earth. Fowl of the air, if little else, had a use for gum-topped box country. It was a rare occasion when snowy plumage and sulphur crests, or crimson bodies and blue wings were not to be seen, either foraging in the foliage or in screeching flight from tree to tree. Here you might disturb a kangaroo-rat from his camp under a tuft of wiry-grass, a fat little bundle of fright who would go bounding down the hillside in ten-feet leaps, with hisses and grunts, evidently under the impression that you were in hot pursuit.

Here – as often in our land – poverty of soil meant growth of wildflowers. There was a thin scattering of pale harebells, and a yellow flower that grew in tight little clumps that looked, from a short distance, like spoonfuls of mustard. There was what looked, for the greater part of the year, like a cartload of old ropes flung over the wreck of a dead tree. I came by in a lucky time and found it a tall cascade of blossom, cream and brown bells. I took a length of it home, hanging over the front of the saddle. Near the top of the slope was a thicket of native hop-bush, knee-high to a rider, ordinarily unnoticeable, but in its season a billow of cream and russet and pale green that brushed about you as you rode through and sent up gusts of warm, tangy sweetness.

The airy crown on the ridge was free of undergrowth, the ground gravelly under a grove of gnarly bloodwood-trees. As you rode along – or stopped to look about you – you could see, through the gaps in the branches, much of the settlement spread out below you, or across the range, or, in another direction, away and away to a faint far shimmering horizon that seemed to lead your thoughts to all the world beyond.

I was on the ridge one day when I became aware of a sustained booming, a prolonged minor roar. There was no wind. I thought of aircraft; then, guided perhaps by a wakening sense of smell, my focus of vision shifted nearer home. The boughs of the bloodwoods were thick with clumps of blossom and loud with native bees.

Going downhill, back toward the sliprails, you came,

after passing through a belt of stunted belah – like a plantation of large Christmas-trees – again to open forest. Ironbark and box, here, with an untidy undergrowth of saplings, cotton-bush and other rubbish. It was dirty country in a settler's way of looking at it, but possums and koalas seemed to like it well. Most of the trees were misshapen and piped, scarcely one but had a branch or two ending in a woody hollow where small furry things might peacefully sleep away the hours of the day. Many of them grew at a slope, and on the bark of the upper surfaces of these you would see, quite plainly, the toe scratches of nocturnal comings and goings.

Against my fence, and just above the sliprails, was a sandalwood slope, small, straight-stemmed trees, with crumbly black bark and many-elbowed branches – as if they had been hard-pruned for years – ending in tough black twigs and a very thin veil of light green leaves. In flowering time their enveloping scent brought thoughts of the fabled Orient, and a thump with the heel of your hand against the trunk would bring groundward a shower of minute pale petals.

A little grass grew here, in scattered tufts, and, although it was a type of country that would scarcely pay for improving, it had a virtue of its own. The thin brown soil was warm. It responded quickly to rain – and to a much lighter rain than would be needed to be effective on heavier country. A day or two after a shower had passed the grass tufts would be like spurts of green flame against the dark moist earth.

On de Burgh's block, as on a great deal of our western

country, irregular rains brought irregular growths, springing the seeds or roots of herbage that had lain dormant in the earth for years, waiting their brief time. I was returning home one nightfall from Tom's place, where I had spent the day helping him to erect a windmill. At the creek-crossing, where the track passed over a half-acre of sandy island, formed by a tiny anabranch, I rode from the sharp eucalyptic tang of the bush into air heavy with garden fragrance. From the night-hidden earth large white flowers were looking up, like a host of apparitional faces. There was a touch of eeriness, of magic, in coming upon this twilight gathering where, my memory of daylight told me, no flowers grew. The feeling remained with me and, nearing the same spot next morning, I was not surprised at seeing no flowers among the tall grass. But, dismounting, I found them, each tight-furled against the light of day. I lingered briefly, squatting on one heel, looking about me, recalling the dim company of the evening before, aware of the inconstancy of our seasons, and knowing that I might not see that fugitive loveliness again inside a dozen years.

For me, de Burgh's block was a place, an escape, and a condition of mind. I went up there, as a rule, when a long bout of toil on my selection had brought me to a physical standstill, and a half-day sitting in the saddle seemed fairly earned. I have spent more than one morning up on the bloodwood ridge with my behind on a cool boulder or a warm one – as the prevailing temperature suggested – and my back against a tree-trunk, reflecting on the folly of labour and the wisdom of idleness.

There was always the excuse of seeing how the heifers

had done during the month or six weeks since last seen. They had a number of night camps: in the scrubby brigalow when a sharp wind blew; beside the waterhole in the dry seasons; and up in the high warm air on the bloodwood ridge of nights when frost was on the creek flats. I think understanding and mutual toleration was arrived at between them and the bush animals. Lying quietly in night camp they would have knowledge of much that took place around them.

By day they might be met anywhere; with their heads down to a tender bite among the sandalwoods, nosing out a green blade or two among the rank brown grass of the creek flat, camped with tight bellies under the apple-box by the waterhole, browsing in the bottle-tree scrub, or standing motionless and without apparent purpose in the arcade of umbrella-brigalow, at the end of one of those walkabouts that cattle running in half-wild country periodically make in response to the urging of obscure emotions.

Wherever they might be, the old horse would rarely be far away. Lacking the companionship of his own species, he identified himself with the heifers, and they, although they had no need of him, granted him a certain measure of social recognition. I have come upon them in camp, he lying in the centre, zoologically confused, it seemed, to the point of thinking he was one of them, but enormously content, nevertheless, and they disposed about him.

And that – unless hands without understanding were laid upon it – was de Burgh's block – last home of the bush animals, the bush, when all the bush at last was vanquished, dwelling-place of the spirit that many have known though none have seen. I knew the last to be true when I rode across what the land maps called Lot 32, one night of preternatural stillness, under a full clear western moon.

De Burgh appeared.

I was at work on my selection. I was carrying my tools out through the scrub track to the front sliprails – which I was replacing with a gate – and had almost reached them when I saw a man pass by the open end of the track. By the time I reached the rails he was twenty yards past them, along the road: a broad-shouldered figure in a cocoa-brown suit. His head was a huge mass of iron-grey curls and he carried a black velour hat in one hand. He was walking, not with the labour-saving slouch of the bushworker, whose body earns his bread, but briskly, as if he had an appointment to keep.

I dropped my tools with a clatter. When I looked up he was coming back. While yet a dozen yards off he beamed and held forth his hand expansively. 'My name is de Burgh,' he cried. 'Simon de Burgh.'

His palm was soft.

He was of striking appearance. In addition to his curls he had a clear sallow skin, big, brown, dreamy, kind-looking eyes under thick iron-grey brows, a horizontal coil of iron-grey moustache above a full-lipped, well-shaped mouth, and a broad chin. He was plump. He looked like a poet in good condition, I thought, or a band-master in mufti.

With a flourish he disclosed a folded land map. 'You'd be my neighbour on Lot 31,' he suggested.

I admitted it.

Without further preliminaries he plunged into a discussion of agricultural topics.

'This land should be good for wheat,' he cried casting an optimistic eye about him.

'It might be all right, if we got regular seasons,' I answered. Something ingenuous in his manner made me wonder if he'd ever seen a bag of wheat except in a suburban fuel and produce store. And I was also imaginatively trying to find a place for a wheat paddock on Lot 32.

'Going in for fodder conservation?' he asked brightly.

He might as well have asked me if I thought of having the paper delivered every morning.

'Not just yet awhile,' I answered.

He spoke of melons in the next breath. At some place he had visited – it was near the coast – he had seen melons that would fill a wheelbarrow; and tomatoes as big as – well, two of them would fill the crown of his hat!

He went on talking like a farmer's weekly. He was full of agricultural chit-chat. He mentioned recent fluctuations in the price of potatoes as if it were a matter of close personal interest to him. He expressed an opinion on the importance of South African maize and another on the export of stud merino rams. He opined that the bull was half the herd. He touched on the troubles that afflict *vignerons* and the handsome rewards accruing to apiarists. He mentioned lucerne! He said that fowls, ducks, and turkeys might be profitable sidelines in our locality. His rural horizon was limitless.

I'd had time to make a further inspection of him and had discovered a rather pathetic difference between his welling enthusiasm and his appearance. His shoes were cracked, his suit had seen a good deal of use and his shirt had very little wear left in it. Also – though this may have been due to weariness after his long walk from the railway – his features drooped a little when he was not actually speaking.

I couldn't shake off the realities of country life as understood in our district sufficiently to make suitable response to his soaring discourse, so I brought him to earth with a couple of personal questions. I learnt that he had selected sight unseen, that he had now come to look over his property for the first time, and that he hoped, with his family, to settle permanently among us a little later on. In return for his information I offered him my good wishes.

We parted soon afterwards with another dramatic handshake and appropriate expressions of mutual goodwill.

I thought a good deal about de Burgh. Strangers mean a lot to you in the bush. After they've gone you go through them with leisurely thoroughness. I could see that for him agricultural production – hens laying eggs, sheep growing wool, grapes yielding wine, land growing crops – was a sort of poetry. But poetry – in living I mean – isn't something you set out to do, it's something you find you did while you were trying like hell to do something else. I imagined de Burgh would be always seeing short-cuts to paradise – and getting bushed trying to follow them. On thinking him over, I found that I liked him – but I couldn't see him in successful occupation of a dry-country selection.

I didn't see him again, but a couple of days later, Tom Howells, with whom he had stayed a night, drove in on his way from taking him to the station. He offered no comment, but there was a twinkle in his eye.

'Do you know what an art and pottery shop is?' he asked.

De Burgh had, at one time, been the proprietor of such an establishment.

At present he was a house-to-house photographer. He'd been editor of a suburban newspaper. He'd written a novel. He'd invented a fly-trap but couldn't get anyone to put any money into it. He'd just missed going with an expedition to the Antarctic. He'd stood for parliament, on an independent ticket.

The materialization of de Burgh and the knowledge of a definite time when he would settle among us dashed my hopes of keeping Lot 32 untouched. Tradition supported the idea that he would eventually abandon it. You'd hear fellows who were on good blocks say of some man who was pursuing a forlorn hope on poor country, 'It's all right. He's improving our land for us', but with the person of de Burgh before my inner eye the day when he would acknowledge defeat seemed too remote to be of interest. Before he gave in he would have hacked Lot 32 to a ruin – and in any case my application would be only one of several.

I had a special reason for the sense of disappointment his arrival had evoked in me. Between my homestead and the front gate lay a twelve or fifteen acre patch of bottle-tree scrub similar to that on de Burgh's block. The track I had cut wound through it. Coming home, after a long drive in the heat, its greenness and shade were like a welcome. More than that. The homestead was built close up to the edge of it, and of summer mornings it threw a cool porch of shadow when the open forest was flooded with scorched gold. At dawn, when the cattle bitch came slapping the side of my bed with her tail to let me know that it was time to show a leg, the birds would be singing along the edge of the scrub. I could hear them through the open window as I pulled my clothes on. I don't mean just a trill or two. They gathered in the scrub near the house from great distances because it was their nearest sheltered approach to water, in the dam at the foot of the slope. From dawn until a little after sunrise the scrub-egde was rowdy with birds. Their song made a pleasant beginning to a day that was often hard enough.

The time was coming when I would have to get into that scrub with axe and firestick, but if de Burgh's block were mine I could afford to let it stand.

Eight months elapsed between the visit of de Burgh and our hearing, through the re-gazettement of the land, of his forfeiture.

I couldn't take the time off to attend the sitting of the land court in Wilgatown, so I appointed the clerk to draw my ballot slip for me. Being a pessimist with a firm belief in the tricks of the devil I made my mind that of the four who were balloting it would go to Paddy McGuire who had more land than enough already. Tom Howells went in to make his own draw.

In the interval of waiting, I told myself I wouldn't think of the matter, so as to forestall disappointment, but I found my thoughts, in spite of me, wandering up to de Burgh's block, putting a fence along the front boundary and damming the lower edge of the little waterhole so that my heifers, paddymelons, possums, and so on, would have a supply of water over even the worst of droughts.

Tom called in on his way back from Wilgatown to tell me – with his friendliest grin – that I was the winner. The strange thing is that as soon as I was in possession of that piece of wasteland, as soon as it was secure from maltreatment, I began to think differently about de Burgh, turning his case over in my mind as I went about my work. I fancied he had found it impossible to finance himself in agricultural enterprise, and wondered what he had turned to. I hoped he was happy in it. On second thoughts I found a lot to admire in him, and was sorry that his hopes and mine should have crossed. It struck me that men like de Burgh have something of the character of Lot 32 – a high resistance to mere practicality. They carry their wasteland inside them.

THE HAIRCUT OF A MORE SUCCESSFUL MAN

NICK EARLS

Ellen doesn't know me, mainly because I tell her so many lies. She knows someone else, a different person I've created and told her about. And I like it better that way. It has so many more possibilities.

She cuts my hair, round about every fourth Saturday. I'm her 11.45, her last appointment. That's a regular thing. She does me like she's in no hurry, as though it's not bad to linger, spend some time in the vicinity of my unspectacular hair, my modest trimming requirements.

It was only a few haircuts into our relationship that I decided I wanted to be a little more glamorous, at least to someone. So when Ellen asked me those hairdresser questions, those broad open-ended How have things been? questions, I really started telling her. And week by week a strange glamour crept into my life, a very measured, downplayed, sophisticated, natural kind of glamour. Stories of considerable, though never boastful, prowess. My work as an international banker, my private adventures.

My trip to Melbourne a few years ago at the time of the Australian Open, meeting Gabriella Sabatini through a mutual friend, playing a set of singles with her. She won six–two and didn't work up a sweat, but four of the games went to deuce.

My lecture tour of the universities of northern Spain, though I never told her what I'd lectured about. My behind-the-scenes work on the Sydney Olympic bid.

Kylie Minogue's twenty-first in '89, the hassles we had with the paparazzi, and the secret name Kylie uses in hotels to screen her calls. And I made this secret part of our relationship, and Ellen swore to tell no-one.

And once she said she'd counted up and she figured I must know at least eleven of the *Who Weekly* list of the world's twenty-five most beautiful people, and she didn't know anyone else who knew even one of them.

So I chose to become a very complex international kind of man, someone very different to the person I could have told her about, the transport economist who drives a ten-year-old Ford Laser and lives alone in a two-bedroom flat a few streets away. And it's a choice I'm usually glad I've made. I'm glad the second or third or fourth time she asked me how things had been I told her about things that were never likely to be.

I ask her about her life, too, and she always prefaces any remarks by telling me it's nowhere near as exciting as mine. She lives over the river where she and her husband Garry are renovating a turn-of-the-century cottage. They have two young daughters, and Garry's always keen for more, and keen for a son or two as well. He just loves kids, she tells me. And it doesn't sound like a bad life at all.

And she washes my hair, washes it slowly before each trim and massages the conditioner deep into my scalp. Works her elegant fingers forcefully into me with a rhythm that sends me into a temporary ecstatic trance. I close my eyes to make the most of every touch. I shut down all other sensations. And she doesn't talk while she's doing this. I think she respects the serene state into which I've drifted and she doesn't do anything that might break it. All the time those fingers, working, working away, working up a lather, rinsing, then hands on again for the conditioner.

And all I can feel is this, all I can see is the dull red inside my eyelids. And I imagine a world where hairdressing is a nude art, where you walk into the salon and the gear comes off, for everybody. So I'm sitting naked with my head tipped back and Ellen working peacefully away. And in this better world my body hair is distributed in a more concise manner, my muscle mass is just a little more impressive and some days I have a dick that would measure up well against the leg of a fat four-year-old child.

In this place only beautiful people cut hair. Ellen still cuts hair there. Ellen with her grey eyes and her straight blonde hair that she dismisses as boring, her breasts loaded into a snug white T-shirt like something dangerous, her black jeans. Nude of course in this other place that only exists while she's washing my hair, her magical liberated breasts dipping down close to my wet head. Breasts growing larger and becoming troublesome, bumping against my head repeatedly like generously inflated balloons, and she's apologising and I'm telling her it's okay, I don't mind. Wet shining large breasts with my head between them.

And she towels me down like a boxing coach and leads me over to the chair. Cuts my hair. Takes the Samson power of my blind, dizzy dream away, just a little. We're both still dressed when I leave.

Sometimes I even want to tell her that I miss her between visits. If I'm having a really shitty time of it I want to go back the next day, just for the wash. But then she'd be onto me for sure.

Sometimes I walk out of there still on a high, hot enough to burn a hole right through my pants, sometimes I'm already crashing down. Walking into the glare of the outside and hating it instantly, all of it. The ugly people who in any better world would never make the grade as hairdressers, the bright raging daylight, the crappy car that I have to leave round the corner where she won't see it, the crappy, brown-brick flat where I'll be parking it, sleeping nights. The place where I watch TV and eat takeaway. Where I drink beer and eat barbecue chips in front of the one-day cricket night games, lounging around on the old sofa night after hot summer night wearing only the haircut of a more successful man. Falling asleep eventually, dreaming the crappy dreams I expect to, waking without enthusiasm.

I think I'm in a rut.

Sometimes I also think I could kill Garry. Garry the daughter-maker. Garry the dream husband. Perfect Garry who found her first. I imagine myself in their leafy suburban street witha sniper's rifle, zeroing the cross hairs in on his chest, blowing him away. I can only think this because I'm far too dull to do it. There are days, though, when it's the first part of a quite unstoppable fantasy. Me lying there on the old sofa with a few beers in me, gazing up at the ceiling and inadvertently making the oral gun noises of childhood.

It's been a while since there has been anyone else in my life, and I suppose that's not surprising if I spend much of my spare time lying around naked drinking beer and fantasising about murdering someone I don't even know. I suppose if I actually did it people would talk about what a quiet neighbour I was, and how they would never have guessed I could have done something like that. But then the *Courier-Mail* would build up a picture of me as some psychotic loner, and this end would come to seem inevitable.

Worse than that, though, it's such a self-defeating fantasy. I shoot the man she loves, Ellen hates me forever, for ten or fifteen years I get a series of very unattractive prison haircuts and it's a long, long time till I come across hands like hers again. And I don't imagine the prison barber works the conditioner into your scalp with any tenderness at all. And I expect it would take a hell of an imagination to fantasise about his breasts enlarging around your wet head. But in times of deprivation, I suppose all such things are possible.

So the fantasy persists, but only on the old sofa, only in my crappy flat. Sometimes I doze while I'm still working on it and a late wicket falls in the night cricket and I'm suddenly awake again. Awake in the flickering lights of replays, still tumescent in the last lingering drift of the dream, still expecting to look down and see a dick like a hot, basking reptile reclining across my belly. But finding instead something more like a moist pink kangaroo baby beginning its slow crawl to the pouch.

The big, bold dreams of lonely men with unimportant dimensions.

When I was young I used to go to a barber with my father. His name was Ron and all he could do was a short back and sides. None of those fancy hairstyles. He was bald and myopic and very ugly in an old-fashioned sort of way. When I worked out, much more recently, that the best hairdressing was done nude, I thought back to Ron the barber. But only once.

In the country of nude hairdressing, Ron would be forever turned back at the border, sent to roam the wilderness with his scissors and his shaving brush, cursing for the rest of his days the cruelties of the world and its unreasonable preoccupation with beauty. And he'd hold up his hands, his stumpy clean little fingers, his tidy nails and he'd moan to the harshly beautiful, grey-eyed goddess of hairdressers, and he'd wail about the land of unseen plenty where they wouldn't even let him get his gear off to shear a few sheep.

I call the salon one Thursday, even though I've seen Ellen just twelve days before. Something big? she says. Yeah, I tell her, and she pencils me in for Saturday, 11.45. I think I might tell her I'm going to Bangkok on Monday because I've found a loop-hole in Thai foreign investment law that will sink a big deal a multi-national is sewing up.

THE HAIRCUT OF A MORE SUCCESSFUL MAN

I have two days to fine-tune the details.

Two days thinking only of Ellen. Two days hard as a bat handle sitting in my one-window office in my senior project officer chair looking out at Spring Hill. Two days thinking only of soap, shampoo, hands in my hair, fuck the traffic lights, fuck the ring-road plans, fuck the minister who wants to take something to cabinet next week. The minister and his ministerial hair, black luxuriant hair always looking well cared for and important. With hair like that, he could be the next premier.

Friday nights is of course a night of precocious masturbation, lying in my long bath in body-temperature water, reasonably well shampooed where it counts. Taking the bat handle and playing several innings of indoor cricket. Afterwards, I sleep quite well, and I wake late.

When I arrive, the salon's still busy dealing with the families lining up in numbers for Saturday morning cuts. Ellen says, Hi babe, in a slightly weary way and goes back to the wriggling blond six-year-old in front of her.

When it's my turn she takes me to the basin. I tell her my hair feels really dirty today, and she says she'll be thorough. She works my head so hard I think I'll moan if I'm not careful. I can't imagine what she'd do if I moaned, because the nature of the moan would be quite apparent. My mouth goes dry at the best of it and I feel quite dizzy. She lifts my head and wraps it in a towel and I can move only slowly to the chair.

Big night? she says.

Yeah. Yeah, fairly big.

How do you want it?

Just a trim. Not much off at all. I just want it to be a little neater.

She doesn't talk as much today. She doesn't initiate conversation in quite the usual way. I see her looking at me sometimes, and I wonder if I moaned, after all.

I ask her how things are and she says, Fine. She doesn't go into any details. Doesn't tell me how the re-wiring's going. Doesn't tell me about Stephanie and Alexandra. Doesn't even tell me about Garry. Maybe somebody's shot him. I should ask.

I don't. I say very little. She doesn't ask me anything, either. This is strange. I almost need to ask her what's going on, but I don't know if I can. And I keep my Thailand story to myself. I know I can't believe it at the moment. Right now I know I stole it from somewhere and it seems like the most transparent of lies, like a lie that could unravel a whole desirable identity. And that'd be it. I'd have to get up and leave with wet partly cut hair and never come back. And Ellen is far too important for me to contemplate that. I realise that now as she's taking millimetres from the ends of my hair, and unless I'm very careful I could become deeply depressed in an instant.

I watch her hands, combing and measuring and trimming. Her face that seems quite far from me today. The reflection of her back view a million times, caught between the mirrors that line both walls.

How's that? she says, when it's done. But she says it as though she's presenting me with nothing, as though it's really just a way of telling me the haircut's over and it's time to go.

Good, really good, I tell her, and in the mirror I'm sure my smile looks unconvincing, perfunctory.

I walk to the cash register. I give her fifteen dollars. She gives me fifty cents. She says, See you next time, then. And I go.

And I feel like shit today, really bad after the cut, like it's got me nowhere. Like the whole weekend is shot, and maybe more. Like the rest of my life is just beer and TV and seasonal sporting fluctuations. So it makes sense that today is the day I lose my car keys. My bulky plastic Captain Haddock keyring that no-one could lose. I am a man facing a ten-year-old white Laser with nothing but his empty pockets, his keys forsaken in some transitional moment. Waiting chair to basin. Basin to cutting hair. Back there, back with Ellen, back where I just can't go right now.

So I stand by the roadside next to my ten-year-old white Laser hoping I will see the blue plastic jumper of Captain Haddock, his slightly startled, bearded, plastic face, lying somewhere on the ground with my keys. Despite my haircut, I feel at this moment very unsuccessful.

Hey.

Ellen's voice says, Hey, just behind me. Says it in a tough kind of way, and I turn. She's different now. A totally different person to the haircutting Ellen at the salon. And she's swinging my Captain Haddock keyring like it's a nunchaku, like, Don't mess with me or the plastic captain will be just a blur when he hits you.

She's crazy and powerful now. She tells me Garry's a shit, stands in this quite busy street and tells me Garry's a shit. That it never worked. That she wanted kids and he just laughed at her and it never looked like happening. She looks at my car, the ten-year-old white Laser I am standing near in a way that says it must be my car. And she says to me, I don't care if it's all lies, okay? I don't give a shit if this isn't the black Saab it's supposed to be. Just get in.

I start to walk to the driver's door and she says, Go round the other side.

She gets in behind the wheel and unlocks the passenger door. I do what I'm told.

Tell me where you live, she says.

I tell her Bishop Street and she says, Right, puts it in gear and drives.

Three and a half minutes it takes. Three and a half minutes of Ellen staring straight ahead. Three and a half minutes of wondering what the hell is going on. It occurs to me, and I don't know why, but it occurs to me that she might be going to kill me. She looks like she could kill me. Maybe she will. Maybe that's fair. I don't know. I know I have an erection of quite fearsome proportions, but it never was a part of my body to show much judgement. The fact that part of me, a small part of me, thinks it's reasonable to have an erection doesn't mean she isn't going to kill me. As though she's read my mind while she's washed my hair, watched every minute of two years of appalling fantasies and today was the day it all became too much and I'm about to get what I deserve.

We park in front of my block of units. It is a visibly crappy block of units, but she says nothing other than Let's go in.

She unlocks the door, shuts it behind us.

I'm putting a lot on the line here, all right? she says. I know you might never come back to me after this.

She's not going to kill me. Maybe the erection wins.

I've been thinking about you, she says, staring out the window with the alarming intensity she's maintained throughout the last six minutes. Even when I'm not cutting your hair. I've been thinking about you and soap. You and me and a shitload of soap. You and me and a lot of shampoo. I've been thinking you might be hairy, she says. Like, really hairy. I've been wanting you to be really hairy, and really in need of a good wash.

I am really hairy, I tell her. Like, really fucking hairy. Hair suit, my friends call me, since they say hirsute doesn't do me justice.

I think this is a joke, but she doesn't laugh.

Garry isn't hairy, she says. Garry has a chest like a boy. Did you get the shampoo I told you to? The Decoré in the flesh-coloured bottle?

Yeah.

We go into the bathroom and start running the water.

Got anything with bubbles? she says.

Yeah, maybe.

She goes to the cupboard and throws a handful of crystals into the bath and it suds up right away, filling the room with the complicated fragrance of flowers of the forest.

She takes my shirt off, then my pants, and tells me to get in.

My God you're hairy she says, with a strange, hungry smile.

Yeah.

She undresses and my dick climbs through the bubbles like a periscope.

She moves on top of me, splashes herself with the warm water and she glistens. She runs the water through her hair and gives me a smile that shows her teeth.

I hope to Christ I'm not going to wake up now to see Steve Waugh being run out. Some crappy highlights package waking me at this moment of exhilaration. Flickering lights, a lonely room, a pointless, raging hard-on.

We'll start with your head, she says. Familiar territory. Then we'll take it one inch at a time.

And she foams the shampoo in my hair with both hands, moves her face closer, her grey eyes, and I see another flash of the white teeth just before her warm wet mouth is onto mine.

She soaps my shoulders, and my chest, rubs handfuls of the suds up and down her own body, breathes heavily. She works her way lower, lower.

Right now I wouldn't care if she did kill me. They'd never get the lid down.

She shampoos between my thighs, rubbing rhythmically from my knees to my groin on both sides. Still crouching over me, straddling me.

And the shampoo runs into my eyes, starts inflicting that stiff pain on them when it runs there and you don't wash it away. And I can't wash it away. I can't move. My eyes start to close and I'm still watching her, hypnotised by her like never before, squatting over me, the foot-long, flesh-coloured bottle of Decoré held right in front of her with both hands, low down and squeezing, squeezing out large amounts of the thick off-white shampoo, squeezing it all over me down there.

And just for a moment, with my near-blinded eyes, this is all very disempowering.

I have no control. None at all.

But I don't care.

Garry is as dead as he needs to be and I didn't have to do a thing. And my crappy flat is right now a far, far better world.

Later we drink beer and eat barbecue chips and lie on the old sofa. Ellen flicks between channels. Old movies, repeats, cricket highlights. Steve Waugh is run out for next to nothing. I don't care.

TV's crap, she says. Tell me a story. I like stories.

FIVE UNUSUAL JOURNEYS

ELIZABETH STEAD

The First Journey
Take one bicycle wheel and push it, either with a hoop or with a rod attached, to the end of a ribbon of road. If the road is silk there may be a yurt at its end. If there is a goat tethered to the yurt and the goat is in need of milking it will be necessary to rest there for one night. The goat must be drained of milk. In the morning it will be permissible to kill the goat and roast its meat in order to be sustained for the remainder of the journey. Before continuing it is essential that the yurt be cleaned and lined with fresh cloth. The remains of the goat must be tied to a tree, in parcels of linen, tied with grass. If linen is unavailable, rice paper will suffice.

To continue along the next road it will be necessary to cross a field of wheat and wade through a stream ... (Be sure to hold the wheel high so it does not touch the water) then turn left. On this road grows a quilt of wild violets, tread carefully and move the wheel gently. Along this road are three small crescents of grass where the traveller may stop and paint the view. Easels are provided and it is perfectly alright to use charcoal. Be sure to tether the wheel to the totem poles provided for this purpose.

Note: If the traveller wishes to wheel slowly along this road until night falls please sleep under the star designated for this purpose.

At the end of this road there is a temple of great age. It is made of crystal. Be sure the eyes are protected when the sun shines through its tower.

The traveller may enter the temple when the sun has reached four o'clock. There is no charge but read the rules carefully. To protect the crystal, the wheel must remain outside the temple – A covering of velvet is advised.

Inside the temple the traveller is not restricted but do not forget to write a postcard and send it to your cat.

The Second Journey

In order to voyage on an ocean one may choose from three modes of travel. These are recommended to those who demand excellence in accommodation, comfort and speed.

The first is the Supreme Ice Floe from the Arctic region. This has the lowest melting capacity of all ice floes. It is furnished with two sheltered deck chairs, ice skates, hockey sticks and a personal sushi chef. Bedding is made from the down of the snow goose. Fur rugs can be hired or purchased during the journey. The Artic Ice Floe will sail the voyager over the oceans of the north and northwest but not so far to the end of the oceans that the floe will slip off the world. The voyager will be encouraged to hesitate at points of interest. A programme of interest includes 'The Killer Whale Hunting' – 'The Seal at the Feast of the Penguin' – A circle of glass on the floe will allow the voyager to view the bottoms of icebergs. 'The Northern Lights' and 'The Longest Night' are available in season. For night blackness, if no stars are visible, candles are provided. Buckets of dead fish and whistles to train dolphins are an optional extra, as are films of the work of Jackson Pollock which can be projected onto ice cliffs. The cost of The Arctic Ice Floe is the price of a heart and the value of its love. Expensive, but to be forever locked in the voyagers' dreams.

The second mode available to the ocean voyager is the medium sized iceberg. These are decorated with alpine plants, friendly fauna and a polar bear family group to keep the hunter amused. There is a small cave excavation for shelter but the bedding is duck down and there is no personal chef. However, pots and pans and instructions for stripping the meat of seals are available and a portion of the ice at the cave's entrance is lime flavoured for the lovers of licks. Fishing tackle may also be purchased but gaffs and nets are an optional extra. Two of this voyage's highlights are the 'Mating of the Terns' and 'Shark Attack' – This medium priced voyage will attract the resourceful, the lithe and those who are fond of the colour green. Cameras are forbidden.

The third option is to journey to the Antarctic ocean in a woollen bag on the deck of a Russian trawler's wheel house. It is not uncomfortable but some work will be expected of the voyager. The voyager will be expected to assist in the repair of nets, peel turnips, dig holes for ice fishing and play the accordion. The voyager may take measurements and count penguins but no parrots are allowed.

The Third Journey
Pack as little as possible in a square of sheer silk and tie the square together with a ribbon of jute. Clothing should be of gauze or muslin – Gossamer should suit very well, if the worms can be persuaded to spin to schedule. Wear a cloak that is diaphanous and will easily float.

Choose a day that is clear and clean with nothing to mist the vision of clouds. The clouds must be white and of sufficient lightness of body to allow for smooth passage across the sky. Clouds that break easily or change their shapes to the likeness of the heads of animals are not recommended. And it is wise not to immediately seek Cloud Nine – it is usually noisy and can sometimes offer only a very short journey. There are many others to choose from.

To choose a cloud, lie on warm, summer grass with your package and watch the sky. Do not forget to wear your cloak and do not look directly at the sun.

When a cloud has been chosen, lie under it and wait for its breeze – (Care should be taken not to choose an Ill Wind – they may try to confuse the traveller but Ill Winds have been clearly marked!). Look for the funnel in the chosen cloud's breeze, this will be indicated by a gentle spiral of grass seed or other small matter rising. Do not be concerned if there are dragonflies, it is a game they play.

Enter the funnel and stand still until you rise with the

aid of the air current and the cloak. Do not forget the silk package.

It will be possible, in some cases, to take a companion but she must be of no greater size than a mouse.

When the chosen cloud has been boarded it may be steered with sky paddles. These are complimentary and may be found next to the picnic basket and the sun hat, stowed at the end that is southern when the cloud is motionless. Also provided are opera glasses and seed to feed the birds. Do not encourage large birds as a cloud can easily be tilted while in motion.

When your cloud is in motion do not try to paddle at a greater speed than the wind. Photography is permitted and especially attractive landscapes will be marked for the convenience of the traveller by tall poles topped with red pennants. Geographical information can be found in the booklet provided.

Do not wave to large aircraft. It can be distracting for the pilots – And avoid hot air balloons.

If the colour of the cloud changes from white to bright red – or to black, it is probably best to shelter behind the moon until normal clouding resumes.

Cloud paddling is for a maximum of one week – with allowances made for unforeseen occurrences.

Cloud gathering is not permitted but the traveller may sing madrigals.

Enjoy.

The Fourth Journey

Take a sled that is light. Make sure the wheels are sound and the chains well greased. Pack the sled with lambs' wool, the underfur of alpaca, tufts of mother hair and weaves of angora. The sled will be lined with kiss curls. These will act as an excellent insulation against the elements. It will be necessary for the occupant to provide his own food and wine glasses. Food should not contain flour, dried fruits or fresh yam. Cake that has risen only with the aid of egg whites is most suitable. Wine, napkins, grape cutters, instruction book, snow maps, avalanche covers and climbing ropes are provided and are to be found in the storage unit under the sled. Clothing should be light and closely woven. Snow caps and ear muffs are an optional extra.

It is advisable that at least two of the travellers have strong legs, for to reach the Top of the World it will be necessary to pedal the wheels of the sled, through snow and ice, to a great height. (The return journey of course requires no pedal power whatever and the traveller will be free to enjoy a glass of wine, the wind in his hair and the thrill of the slide!) – Pedals are situated on both sides of the sled, towards the front. Auxiliary pedals are provided and may be fitted to the rear of the sled if additional power is needed. The instruction book will give the traveller full installation details, with diagrams. Do not forget to detach the auxiliary wheel before returning from the Top of the World.

When the traveller has reached his destination, and provided there is not too much cloud below the peak and the snow is not too blinding, it will be possible, for a small charge, to have his portrait painted in oils, standing triumphant and waving the red signal flags provided by the artist. For an additional charge the traveller may have his likeness inserted into a snow dome. These are very popular.

Do not forget to tie the sled firmly to the poles marked for this purpose.

It is possible that the traveller will be a little short of breath so that pipe smoking and the inhalation of related substances is not recommended.

Do not take advantage of the artist and his family. While they will appear to be hospitable it is inadvisable to enter their home. If hot water is required for tea it is wise to offer a rupee or two for the service.

Do not stay on The Top of the World for more than four hours. If the traveller does not carry a timepiece the artist will blow his horn to signal that the time has expired.

At the completion of the return journey the traveller is asked to leave the sled in its designated stall and to make sure it is left as the traveller found it.

Be sure to gather your own furs and see that the kiss curls are dry.

This journey is not recommended for travellers over the age of forty-eight or for Geminis.

If the traveller wishes, it is permissible to take a television crew on the journey but the traveller must bear entirely the costs involved.

Responsibility is taken only for the traveller's enjoyment.

The Fifth Journey

Take a pole with five Chinese lanterns hung from it, and a basket that is able to be hung from the head or the shoulder. A minimum of clothing that is easily detached should be worn.

Do not light the lanterns until the end of an Underpath has been reached.

To find an Underpath it will be necessary to journey to the part of your world that is blessed by mountains. They need not form a chain or be so high that they are peaked with ice but there must be one mountain that is crowned by an aura of blue light. It is at the foot of this mountain that the traveller will find an Underpath.

The beginning of an Underpath will be marked for the traveller's convenience by a young boy whose job it is to point. A gratuity is not necessary.

At this stage it is wise to check the lanterns for tears or faults, and the basket for The Underpath Guide, pillow and musical scores. No food or beverage is permitted on this journey.

An Underpath will be constructed of damp leaf matter and moss and the traveller will be wise to remove his slippers to avoid slippage ... (The traveller already will have signed the 'no liability' form and will know that while all care is taken during this journey there is no responsibility for frivolous actions).

Follow the Underpath with care, it will be straight and narrow. Do not be tempted to detour to Upthegardenpath or the Wrongpath, both of which have been clearly marked but may be disguised.

At the end of the Underpath there will be the entrance to The Caves. The traveller's tickets of entry will be at the entrance under the black rock.

At this point, read the Guide carefully. It will be necessary for the traveller to remove his clothes, place them in the basket and light the lanterns. A flame for this purpose is situated near the black rock. There is no additional charge for this but see that the flame is alive when replaced.

Safety glasses are also available but these are an optional extra.

Inside the cave the traveller will see five stairways that spiral downwards. These are furnished with illuminated glass hand rails for safety. Refer to the map in the Underpath Guide. It will suggest that it is best not to journey straight to the Grand Chamber but to explore the three smaller alcoves and the Soul Grotto first. It is recommended that the traveller begins with the stairway on his left.

Please descend quietly so as not to wake the bats.

In the first alcove the traveller will find a string trio. Please do not speak to the musicians. If the traveller requires Beethoven tap the lantern pole twice but gently on the floor of the cave. For Elgar, it is three taps (for other selections refer to the Underpath Guidebook) – It is permissible to take the pillow from the basket and sit on it for the duration of the performance. Applause is not permitted.

In the second and third alcoves the traveller will find a pianist and an organ-grinder. As in alcove one, lantern pole signals must be repeated for performance requests. Applause is not permitted.

In the Soul Grotto the traveller may choose from one

of two chamber orchestras or the final act of an opera (Regrettably, *Aida* has been discontinued due to circumstances beyond control).

In the Soul Grotto, because of its greater size, it is possible for the traveller to place his pillow on one of the many tiered and hand carved stone seats.

In the Soul Grotto it is necessary to signal choice of performance by waving the lanterns in the patterns described in the Underpath Guide.

Drinking water may be obtained from pools behind the seat tiers. There is no charge.

At the end of a performance a sign of appreciation by briskly rubbing the palms of the hands together is permitted.

Before entering the Grand Chamber the traveller is advised to place the basket and the lanterns in a niche provided but to carry the pillow. The seating is similar to that in the Soul Grotto but a thousand times more extensive. Carefully note your position in the Chamber and the position of its entry and exit. The vast roof of the Chamber is alight with the firetails of cavern creatures and though the traveller will find this enchanting, photography, sketching or painting is not permitted.

The Grand Chamber contains a full symphony orchestra and a human choir of three hundred and eighty-nine. A continuous programme of Mahler, Berlioz, Wagner and Verdi (in season) is performed and personal requests will be ignored. At the end of these performances applause is permitted and cave bats, autographed by the conductor, will be on sale by the exit. A fitting finale and memento for the traveller, particularly for those in possession of a scrap book.

Clothing may now be worn but do not extinguish the lanterns until once more on the Underpath.

This is a highly emotional journey and not recommended for the depressed or those who cannot sing.

No pets of any kind are allowed.

Brava!

CLOSER

DAVID MALOUF

There was a time, not so long ago, when we saw my Uncle Charles twice each year, at Easter and Christmas. He lives in Sydney but would come like the rest of us to eat at the big table at my grandmother's, after church. We're Pentecostals. We believe that all that is written in the Book is clear truth without error. Just as it is written, so it is. Some of us speak in tongues and others have the gift of laying on hands. This is a grace we are granted because we live as the Lord wishes, in truth and charity.

My name is Amy, but in the family I am called Ay, and my brothers, Mark and Ben, call me Rabbit. Next year, when I am ten, and can think for myself and resist the influences, I will go to school like the boys. In the meantime my grandmother teaches me. I am past long division.

Uncle Charles is the eldest son, the firstborn. When you see him in family photographs with my mother and Uncle

James and Uncle Matt, he is the blondest; his eyes have the most sparkle to them. My mother says he was always the rebel. She says his trouble is he never grew up. He lives in Sydney, which Grandpa Morpeth says is Sodom. This is the literal truth, as Aaron's rod, which he threw at Pharaoh's feet, did literally become a serpent and Jesus turned water into wine. The Lord destroyed Sodom and he is destroying Sydney, but with fire this time that is slow and invisible. It is burning people up but you don't see it because they burn from within. That's at the beginning. Later, they burn visibly, and the sight of the flames blistering and scorching and blackening and wasting to the bone is horrible.

Because Uncle Charles lives in Sodom we do not let him visit. If we did, we might be touched. He is one of the fools in Israel – that is what Grandpa Morpeth calls him. He has practised abominations. Three years ago he confessed this to my Grandpa and Grandma and my Uncle James and Matt, expecting them to welcome his frankness. Since then he is banished, he is as water spilled on the ground that cannot be gathered up again. So that we will not be infected by the plague he carries, Grandpa has forbidden him to come on to the land. In fact, he is forbidden to come at all, though he does come, at Easter and Christmas, when we see him across the home-paddock fence. He stands far back on the other side and my grandfather and grandmother and the rest of us stand on ours, on the grass slope below the house.

We live in separate houses but on the same farm, which is where my mother and Uncle James and Uncle Matt, and Uncle Charles when he was young, grew up, and where my Uncles James and Matt still work.

They are big men with hands swollen and scabbed from the farm work they do, and burnt necks and faces, and feet with toenails grey from sloshing about in rubber boots in the bails. They barge about the kitchen at five o'clock in their undershorts, still half asleep, then sit waiting for Grandma to butter their toast and pour their tea. Then they go out and milk the herd, hose out the bails, drive the cows to pasture and cut and stack lucerne for winter feed — sometimes my brothers and I go with them. They are blond like Uncle Charles, but not so blond, and the hair that climbs our above their singlets, under the adam's apple, is dark. They are jokers, they like to fool about. They are always teasing. They have a wild streak but have learned to keep it in. My mother says they should marry and have wives.

Working a dairy farm is a healthy life. The work is hard but good. But when I grow up I mean to be an astronaut.

Ours is a very pleasant part of the country. We are blessed. The cattle are fat, the pasture's good. The older farmhouses, like my grandfather's, are large, with many rooms and wide verandahs, surrounded by camphor-laurels, and bunyas and hoop-pines and Scotch firs. Sodom is far off, but one of the stations on the line is at the bottom of our hill and many trains go back and forth. My Uncle Charles, however, comes by car.

His car is silver. It is a BMW and costs an arm and a leg. It has sheepskin seat covers and a hands-free phone. When Uncle Charles is on the way he likes to call and announce his progress.

The telephone rings in the hallway. You answer. There

are pips, then Uncle Charles says in a jokey kind of voice: 'This is GAY 437 calling. I am approaching Bulahdelah.' The air roaring through the car makes his voice sound weird, like a spaceman's. Far off. It is like a spaceship homing in.

Later he calls again. 'This is GAY 437,' the voice announces. 'I am approaching Wauchope.'

'Don't any one of you pick up that phone,' my grandfather orders.

'But, Grandpa,' my brother Ben says, 'it might be Mrs McTaggart.' Mrs McTaggart is a widow and our neighbour.

'It won't be,' Grandpa says. 'It will be him.'

He is a stranger to us, as if he had never been born. This is what Grandpa says. My grandmother says nothing. She was in labour for thirty-two hours with Uncle Charles, he was her first. For her, it can never be as if he had never been born, even if she too has cast him out. I heard my mother say this. My father told her to shush.

You can see his car coming from far off. You can see it *approaching*. It is very like a spaceship, silver and fast; it flashes. You can see its windscreen catching the sun as it rounds the curves between the big Norfolk Island pines of the golf course and the hospital, then its flash flash between the trees along the river. When it pulls up on the road outside our gate there is a humming like something from another world, then all four windows go up of their own accord, all together, with no one winding, and Uncle Charles swings the driver's door open and steps out.

He is taller than Uncle James or Uncle Matt, taller even

than Grandpa, and has what the Book calls beautiful locks. They are blond. 'Bleached,' my grandfather tell us. 'Peroxide!' He is tanned and has the whitest teeth I have ever seen.

The corruption is invisible. The fire is under his clothes and inside him, hidden beneath the tan.

The dogs arrive, yelping. All bunched together, they go bounding over the grass to the fence, leaping up on one another's backs with their tails wagging to lick his hands as he reaches in to fondle them.

'Don't come any closer,' my grandfather shouts. 'We can see you from there.'

His voice was gruff, as if he had suddenly caught cold, which in fact he never does, or as if a stranger was speaking for him. Uncle Charles has broken his heart. Grandpa has cast him out, as you cut off a limb so that the body can go on living. But he likes to see that he is still okay. That it has not yet begun.

And in fact he looks wonderful – as far as you can see. No marks.

Once when he got out of the car he had his shirt off. His chest had scoops of shadow and his shoulders were golden and so smooth they gave off a glow. His whole body had a sheen to it.

Uncle James and Uncle Matt are hairy men like Esau, they are shaggy. But his chest and throat and arms were like an angel's, smooth and polished as wood.

You see the whiteness of his teeth, and when he takes off his sunglasses the sparkle of his eyes, and his smoothness and the blondness of his hair, but you do not se the marks. This is because he does not come close.

My grandmother stands with her hands clasped, and breathes but does not speak. Neither does my mother, though I have heard her say to my father, in an argument: 'Charlie's just a big kid. He never grew up. He was always such fun to be with.'

'Helen!' my father said.

I know my grandmother would like Uncle Charles to come closer so that she could really see how he looks. She would like him to come in and eat. There is always enough, we are blessed. There is an ivory ring with his initial on it, C, in the dresser drawer with the napkins, and when we count the places at table she pretends to make a mistake, out of habit, and sets one extra. But not the ring. The place stays empty all through our meal. No one mentions it.

I know it is Grandpa Morpeth's heart that is broken, because he has said so, but it is Grandma Morpeth who feels it most. She likes to touch. She is always lifting you up and hugging. She does not talk much.

When we go in to eat and take up our napkins and say grace and begin passing things, he does not leave; he stays there beside his car in the burning sunlight. Sometimes he walks up and down outside the fence and shouts. It is hot. You can feel the burning sweat on him. Then, after a time, he stops shouting and there is silence. Then the door of his car slams and he roars off.

I would get up if I was allowed and watch the flash flash of metal as he takes the curves round the river, past the hospital, then the golf course. But by the time everyone is finished and we are allowed to get down, he is gone. There is just the wide green pasture, open and empty, with clouds making giant shadows and the trees by the river in a silvery shimmer, all their leaves humming a little and twinkling as they turn over in a breeze that otherwise you might not have felt.

Evil is in the world because of men and their tendency to sin. Men fell into error so there is sin, and because of sin there is death. Once the error has got in, there is no fixing it. Not in this world. But it is sad, that, it is hard. Grandpa says it has to be; that we must do what is hard to show that we love what is good and hate what is sinful, and the harder the thing, the more love we show Him.

But I don't understand about love any more than I do about death. It seems harder than anyone can bear to stand on one side of the fence and have Uncle Charles stand there on the other. As if he was already dead, and death was stronger than love, which surely cannot be.

When we sit down to our meal, with his chair an empty space, the food we eat has no savour. I watch Grandpa Morpeth cut pieces of meat with his big hands and push them between his teeth, and chew and swallow, and what he is eating, I know, is ashes. His heart is closed on its grief. And that is what love is. That is what death is. Us inside at the table, passing things and eating, and him outside, as if he had never been born; dead to us, but shouting. The silver car with its dusky windows that roll up of their own accord and the phone in there in its cradle is the chariot of death, and the voice announcing, 'I am on the way, I am approaching Gloucester, I am approaching Taree' – what can that be but the angel of death?

The phone rings in the house. It rings and rings. We pause at the sink, in the middle of washing up, my grandmother and my mother and me, but do not look at one another. My grandfather says: 'Don't touch it. Let it ring.' So it keeps ringing for a while, then stops. Like the shouting.

This Easter for the first time he did not come. We waited for the telephone to ring and I went out, just before we sat down to our meal, to look for the flash of his car along the river. Nothing. Just the wide green landscape lying still under the heat, with not a sign of movement in it.

That night I had a dream, and in the dream he did come. We stood below the verandah and watched his car pull up outside the fence. The smoky windows went up, as usual. But when the door swung open and he got out, it was not just his shirt he had taken off, but all his clothes, even his shoes and socks. Everything except his sunglasses. You could see his bare feet in the grass, large and bony, and he glowed, he was smooth all over, like an angel.

He began to walk up to the fence. When he came to it he stood still a moment, frowning. Then he put his hand out and walked on, walked right through it to our side, where we were waiting. What I thought, in the dream, was that the lumpy coarse-stemmed grass was the same on both sides, so why not? If one thick blade didn't know any more than another that the fence was there, why should his feet?

When he saw what he had done he stopped, looked back at the fence and laughed. All around his feet, little daisies and gaudy, bright pink clover flowers began to appear, and the petals glowed like metal, molten in the sun but cool, and spread uphill to where we were standing, and were soon all around us and under our shoes. Insects, tiny grasshoppers, sprang up and went leaping, and glassy snails no bigger than your little fingernail hung on the grass stems, quietly feeding. He took off his sunglasses, looked down at them and laughed. Then looked across to where we were, waiting. I had such a feeling of lightness and happiness it was as if my bones had been changed into clouds, just as the tough grass had been changed into flowers.

I knew it was a dream. But dreams can be messages. The feeling that comes with them is real, and if you hold on to it you can make the rest real. So I thought: if he can't come to us, I must go to him.

So this is what I do. I picture him. There on the other side of the fence, naked, his feet pressing the springy grass. *Stretch out your hand*, I tell him. *Like this*. I stretch my hand out. *If you have faith, the fence will open for you, as the sea did before Moses when he reached out his hand.* He looks puzzled. No, I tell him, *don't think about it. Just let it happen.*

It has not happened yet. But it will. Then, when he is close at last, when he has passed through the fence and is on our side, I will stretch out my hand and touch him, just under the left breast, and he will be whole. He will feel it happening to him and laugh. His laughter will be the proof. I want this more than anything. It is my heart's desire.

Each night now I lie quiet in the dark and go over it.

The winding up of the smoky windows of the chariot of death. The swinging open of the door. Him stepping out and looking towards me behind his sunglasses. Me telling him what I tell myself:

Open your heart now. Let it happen. Come closer, closer. See? Now reach out your hand.

ALL THOSE BLOODY YOUNG CATHOLICS

HELEN GARNER

Watto! Me old darling. Where have you been. Haven't seen you since ... Let me buy you a drink. Who's your mate? Jan. Goodday Jan. What'll it be, girls? Gin and tonic, yeah. Lemon squash. Fuckin' – well, if that's what you. Hey mate. Mate. Reluctant barmen round here. Mate. Over here. A gin and bloody nonsense, a scotch and water for myself, and a – Jesus Mary and Joseph – *lemon squash*. I know. I asked her but that's what she wanted. Well and how's the world been treating you Watto me old mate. No, not a blue. I was down the Yarra last week in the heat, dived in and hit a snag. Gerry? Still in Perth. I saw him not so long ago, still a young pup, still a young man, a young Apollo, a mere slip of a lad. I went over to Perth. I always wanted to go over. I've been everywhere of course in Australia, hate to hear those young shits telling me about overseas, what's wrong with here? anyway what? yeah well I've got this mate who's the secretary of the bloody Waterside Workers, right? I says to him, think I'll slip over to Perth. He says, Why don't you go on a boat? I says, What? How much? Don't shit me, he says. For you – nothin'. Was I seasick? On the Bight? No fear. Can't be seasick when you're as drunk as. Can't be the two at the same time. All those seamen drunk, playin' cards, tellin' lies – great trip, I tell you great trip. Course I got off at the other end had a bit of trouble, once you're back on dry land the booze makes itself felt, but anyway there I was. Yeah yeah, I'm gettin' to Gerry. Blokes on the boat asked me where I was goin', I says, Don't worry, I've got this mate, he works at the university – I didn't tell 'em he was a bloody senior – what is it? senior lecturer? Reader. Anyway first bloke I run into was this other mate, Jimmy Clancy, you'd remember him I suppose, wouldn't like him. bi-i-ig strong bloke, black beard, the lot, always after the women, well he hasn't changed, still running after 'em, I told him off, I lectured him for an hour. Anyway it was great to see him again. He used to hang around with Laurie Driscoll, Barney O'Brien, Vincent Carroll, Paddy Sheehan, *you* know. Paddy Sheehan? Pad hasn't had a drink in – ooh, must be eight years. He was hittin' it before, though. Tell you about Pad. I was in Sydney not so long ago, went up for the fight, well, on the way home I went through Canberra and I tell you it was shockin'. Yeah I said *shockin'*. Ended up in a sort of home for derelicts – the Home for Homeless Men! Well, I come to out there, I had plenty of money see, it was the fight, the time Fammo beat Whatsisname up Sydney, I had tons of money, tons of it, I says to this Christian bloke out there – he wasn't one of those rotten Christians, he was one of the ones with heart – I says to him, Listen mate, I don't want to stay here, I've got plenty of money, just get me out of here – I've got this mate Paddy Sheehan who's a government secretary or something, so the bloke comes out to pick me up in a bloody chauffeur-driven car, bloke in front with a peaked cap and that, Paddy with his little white freckly face sitting up in the back in his glory – he really laid it on for me. So I says goodbye to the Christian bloke, I says Here, have some of this and I give him some money. How much? Oh I dunno, I had handfuls of it, it was stickin' out of me pockets, I just passed him a handful of notes and away I went in the big black car. All right all right, I'm gettin' to Gerry. Perth wasn't I. Yeah well we sat and we talked of the times that are gone, with all the good people of Perth looking on. Ha ha! Course we did. He's still a boy, full of charm, like a son to me. He was a young tough buck then, love, all handsome and soft, wet behind the ears, and Watto here done the dirty on him, didn't you Watto! Yes you did, you broke his heart, and he was only a boy, yes sweetheart – what was your name again? Watto here she hates me to tell this story, yes she does! He was only a child, straight out of a priestery – no, must have been a monkery because he said he had to wear sandals – course he'd never fucked in his life! Didn't know what to do with his prick! And Watto here goes through him like a packet of salts! Makes mincemeat out of him! Poor bloke never knew what hit him. Drove us all crazy with his bloody guitar playing. She told him didn't you Watto that she didn't want no bloody husband but he wouldn't listen, he was besotted, drawin' her pictures, readin' her the poems of W.B. Yeats, playin' his flamin' guitar – they used to fuck all day and all night, I swear to you love – no shutup Watto! it's true isn't it! I dunno what the other young Catholics in the house thought was goin' on in there – but one day I gets this lettuce and I opens their door a crack and I shoves the lettuce through and I yells out, If you fuck like rabbits you better eat like 'em too! He he! Look at her blush! Ah Watto weren't they great times. Drinkin' and singin' and fightin' over politics. I remember a party at Mary Maloney's place when Laurie Driscoll spewed in the back yard and passed out – next morning at home he wakes up without his false teeth – he had to call poor Mary and get her to go out in the garden and poke around and see if he hadn't left his teeth behind as well as the contents of his guts. Oh, all those bloody young Catholics – 'cept for Gerry, who was corrupted by Watto here – don't get me wrong Wats! you done him a favour – they were all as pure as the driven snow – dyin' of lust but hangin' on like grim death for marriage, ha ha! They thought they were a fire-eatin' mob in those days but they're all good family men now. Course, *I* was never allowed to bring no women home, bloody Barney he tells me, Don't you dare bring those hooers of yours back here, you old dero – I had to sneak them round the lane and into me loft out the back. And finally Watto here gives young Gerald the khyber, he moons tragically for weeks till we're all half crazy – and then he met Christine. *Byoodiful.* Wasn't she Watto. *Byoodiful* ... ah ... she's still me best mate. Gerry was that keen to impress her the first time he got her to come back to our place, he says to me, Now you stay away, I don't want no foul language, she's a lovely girl. So I stays away and that night I come back real late from the Waiters' Club with this sheila and we're up in the loft and in the morning I didn't know how I was goin' to get her out of there! They were all down in the yard doin' their bloody exercises, Barney and Dell and Derum – so in despair I pushes her out the door of the loft and she misses the ladder and falls down into the yard and breaks both her flamin' legs. Lucky Barney was a final year medical student. Oh Christine was beautiful though – I'll never forget the night you and her brought Gerry back here, Watto, he was that drunk, he'd been found wallowing with his guitar in the flowerbeds outside that girls' dormitory joint you two lived in – youse were draggin' him along between you and he was singin' and laughin' and bein' sick – and then you went off, Watto, and left the poor young girl stranded with this disgusting drunk on her hands! Laugh! Aaahhhhh. Course much later she goes off with Chappo. I remember the night she disappeared. And years after *that* she took off with that show pony McWatsisname, McLaughlin. Didn't you know that? Yeah, she went off with him – course, she's livin' with someone else now. Oh, a beautiful girl. Gorgeous. They fought over her, you know. They fought in the pub, and bloody McLaughlin had a fuckin' aristotle behind his back while poor Chappo had his fists up honourable like this – I got the bottle off McLaughlin. At least if you blue you should do it proper. Cut it out, I says, look you don't have to fight over cunt! If I was to fight over every sheila I'd ever fucked there'd be fights from here to bloody Darwin! Why do they have to fight over them? Those bloody young Catholics. Gerry. All right all right. And fighting over women! You don't have to *fight* for it! Look if I can't get a fuck there's a thousand bloody massage parlors between here and Sydney, I can go into any one of them and get myself a fuck, without having to *fight* for it. I never put the hard word on you, did I Watto, in all those years? Well, Gerry. Yeah, he was in great form, lovely boy, always felt like a father to him, I taught him everything he knew, I brought him up you might say. Oh, he's been over London and all over the place but he's back over the west now, just the same as ever. Aaaah Watto I've been in love with you for twenty years. Go on. It must be that long. Look at her – turns away and giggles. Well, fifteen then. You're looking in great shape. Gerry. Yeah, yeah ... he was a lovely boy. Don't I remember some story about you and him in Perth once? Something about a phone box in the middle of the night? Oh. Right. I'll stop there. Not a word more. You're lookin' in great shape Watto. Your tits are still little though aren't they. How's the baby, my girlfriend? How old is she now? *Nine*. Jeesus Christ. She still goin' to marry me? I seen her come in here lookin' for your old man one time, he was drinkin' in here with some of the old crowd, she comes in the door there and looks round and spots him. Comes straight up to him and says, Come home! And bugger me if he doesn't down his drink and get up and follow her out the door as meek as a lamb. *Pleeez* sell no more drink to my father / It makes him so strange an' so wild ... da da dummm ... / Oh pity the poor drunkard's child. A real little queen. Imagine the kid you and I would have had together eh Watto – one minute swingin' its little fists smashin' everything, next minute mai poetry, mai music, mai drawing! Schizo. Aaah Jesus. Have another drink. You're not going? Ah stay! I only ever see you once every five years. Give us a kiss then. I always did love ya. Ha ha! Don't thank me. Happy New Year and all the best. Ta ta.

PIPE DREAM

CHANDANI LOKUGÉ

Priya is ten years old and lives with his family by the sea. He has two elder sisters, a younger brother and a younger sister. Often he sits idle on the beach and stares into the sea. He is always hungry and this somewhat restricts his movements. He has one pair of shorts. His skinny chest is bare, always.

I would walk up to him. And? And why not?

But here is someone else. An old white man. A tourist, his skin burnt red in the sun. He wears a skimpy pair of red bathers and a large silver wrist watch. The child is still unaware of the other presence, and looks towards the sea. He has tried to draw a letter or two on the wet sand with his fingers. He remembers them from his few sporadic terms in school. The letters are unformed and will soon be erased from sand and memory. The waves smash against rock. The sun is a searing eye in the cloudless sky. The child is small and unprotected on the shore. And hungry.

Priya is not unused to tourists. They swarmed all over the beach during this season. His eldest sister, Maya, had a half-white-half-brown child that lay on the floor in a corner of the hut. Its father was unknown. Maya had revealed nothing, not even after their father beat her up and kicked her against the wall when she was pregnant. But no one had expected a half-breed. Everyone was ashamed of it, even Priya. Some of his friends understood, however. He was not the only one in such a situation. The little half-breed was over two months old. But it had no name. Priya's mother wished that it would die, everyone knew that. It was undernourished anyway and would whimper the day away on a threadbare mat until she yelled at him to 'throw the pariah in the sea'. He would then lift it clumsily in his arms. He would be careful not to take it out of the hut where a neighbour could see it and comment about its birth and about the character of its mother. Occasionally, hurt by the wrinkled red face and large sad eyes, Priya would put his finger in its searching mouth and let it suck suck suck. And be quietened for a while. He wished Maya would return home. But she had run away soon after the birth of the baby and had left no trace. Priya though it was unfair of her to have left the infant behind, motherless, fatherless and foodless.

He himself missed Maya. He missed the affection that she showered on him. He could see her now in her clinging red dress, returning home late from somewhere after their father had sailed away to sea. Sometimes she brought him a bulto from the tea boutique. Often she would swing him off the ground and swirl him round and round, until, tangled in the long tresses of her hair and in the red folds of her skirt, they would fall laughing in a heap on the soft sand. When she was in good humour, and there was a lull in the wind, she would call him behind the house, mix a bit of soap in water, dip a papaw stem in it and blow rainbow bubbles for him. He loved to watch them float away, far far away. In the chilly nights he would curl into her warmth and she would grumble a bit but cover him with her cloth. Then one day she went away and never came back. Perhaps she had walked into the sea. Their mother cursed the day that she had been born and said she would burn forever in hell. But she reserved a decade in her rosary for Maya. The hurt of Maya stings Priya's heart.

The old white man says hello to Priya. Startled out of his inarticulate reflections Priya stares at him without friendliness. The man's eyes gauge the thin body, and he almost moves away. But for his liquid eyes, the child is not attractive. But then, neither is he. He hesitates to approach the bigger boys or the pimps because they might make fun of his sagging body, his age. The wrist watch glints brilliantly in Priya's eyes and blinds him for the moment. Had he been bigger and stronger he might have grabbed the watch and run. It would have fed his family for a week. As it is, he knows that the effort would be useless. 'Where do you live?' the man asks and Priya points out one of the huts that lines the beach behind them. Even as they watch, his mother comes out of the hut in a rush, turns some bits of salted fish drying in the sun, tightens her cloth around her waist and goes in. Had she seen him, she might have called to him. She knew what these old white men were. But she is busy and has no time to look. You can understand that. Priya's younger brother and sister and Maya's half-breed claimed all her attention during the day.

The man surveys the scene: fishermen rest here and there against the sides of catamarans dragged on shore, after their night at sea and the early morning haul and distribution of fish. Many of them are bleary eyed with toddy. A mangy dog slinks about in search of scraps and is sometimes kicked. Now and then someone picks up a strand of baila. But it hardly catches on. For the majority, the night has been unsuccessful and there is a sense of tiredness, of defeated will. After the Mudalali claimed his share of the haul, there is sometimes, like today, nothing at all to sell. Just a few under-sized cheap fish that the women might cook for the family later in the afternoon. At this time of mid-morning, a few of the luckier women are ambling back home with empty baskets after quick sales in residential areas, others tend their children, wash pots or just sit around picking lice and gossiping. The old white man dismisses them contemptuously and turns back to the boy.

'Want to come with me? I have chocolates and cigarettes,' he says in English. Priya understands chocolates and cigarettes. He also has a vague idea about why the man offered them to him. A number of the boys he hung around with smoked foreign cigarettes, traded foreign chocolates and chewing gum, and wore shiny nylon shirts and wrist watches. They also made subtle jokes about how they came about such goodies. Often he would guffaw with them even though he hardly understood their meaning. His mother was aware of these goings on. And she threatened him daily. She swore she should burn his legs or beat him until he could never walk again if she found him in a sudda's net. 'Do you hear me?' she would ask him, tweaking his ear, after she had completed such a tirade. 'Yes amme', he said to her each time. When she was not too tired in the nights she would make him kneel with her by the Mary-and-Child-Jesus picture that adorned the inner wall of their hut. When she had oil in the house she would carefully measure out a lid-full into the small glass lamp that sat in front of the picture and light the wick. The dim flame would light up the red of Mary's cheeks, her tranquil lips and the gold dusted skin of the baby Jesus. Sleepily Priya would stare at the picture and think to himself that the baby Jesus was a plumped up, dimpled version of their Maya's baby. Often, before his mother finished saying her rosary, Priya would curl up on the floor at her feet. At last, she would bend down to lift him up and lay him a few feet away by the baby. Then Priya occasionally wrapped his arms around her neck and gazed at her with eyes that held dreams. He was the baby Jesus who suffused her face with Mary's glow.

Now, Priya looks back towards the hut undecided. He has eaten nothing today but a slice of dry bread. His hunger will grow with the day and when he returns home at dinner time, his mother will ask him why he could not earn some money by mending a net or repairing a boat. She never meant what she said and usually doled out a spoonful of rice for him with a bit of fish curry or shredded coconut. She knows he is too weak and timid for anything but school. He could not even sell a shell or a garland of beads to a tourist without a bigger boy cuffing him on the head and grabbing the money from him. But who could afford the books and the clothes? His father thinks he should be employed as a servant in the Mudalali's bungalow. After Maya's scandal, the good sisters at the convent had found a place for Soma, Priya's other elder sister. But that was in a respectable home. Whenever she dwelt on Priya in the Mudalali's bungalow, however, the mother's blood ran cold. Everyone knew the Mudalali was a shark who toiled his fishermen to the bone. So she postponed the decision.

Priya craved daily for the chocolates that the bigger boys munched in front of his eyes in the evenings. He would trail them obsessively. Occasionally, they remembered to throw him a titbit that he tossed down without tasting. The old white man looks at the skinny child, at his naked chest and narrow hips from which his shorts, several sizes too large for him, hang down. His eyes blur and his lips thicken lasciviously. He points to his wrist watch and holds it out. He begins to walk away. He knows that the child has little choice, that he must succumb. If not today, then tomorrow or the day after.

And the child follows. The child follows. But he looks back often.

The white man lives in a cabana some distance away from the line of fishing huts. Priya has never entered a cabana before. Anything could scare him away. The man knows this. And for the moment he does not talk. He just walks up the steps on to the narrow balcony and heaves into the chaise longue. It is cooler here than on the beach.

Coconut fronds wave gently and weave crisscross shadows on the balcony. Priya looks about him timidly. From where he stands he can see into the bed room. On the bed side table are the promised chocolates, the cigarettes and the chewing gum. There is also a bowl of fruit. Priya licks his dribbling lips. The man's eyes follow the child's. 'Not yet, not yet,' he says, now confident of conquest. After a while he stands up, looks around the beach furtively and walks into the house. 'Come,' he says, to Priya as he crosses the door-way. Priya hesitates now that the actual moment is before him. Fear wells up in him. He half turns to go back. Perhaps his mother is already combing the beach for him. The man is knowing and crafty. He holds out a chocolate from the bedroom. Priya moves towards it. The man closes the door behind them and drops the chocolates back in the bowl.

The man sits on the bed. He draws Priya to him and begins to fondle his unformed body. Priya squirms but tries to smile and to please, his attention still centred on the bed side table. He is also excited that he has been employed at last to do the work of the big boys. The man is gentle at first. Gradually the morning's hunger and the appeasing chocolates recede. Priya is suspended in a soap bubble magically gliding away, far far away. But suddenly the man turns Priya around violently, and pushes him down on the bed. The pain strikes and drives relentlessly through the body. The man yanks back Priya's head and clamps down on his mouth. All is silent but for the rasping gasp of breath. Priya's stiffened stick legs protrude from the bed. The man impales him with harsh abrupt scathing thrust. The pain swells and surges. And then: cessation.

The smell as of crushed flowers spills into the ensuing stillness. A fly begins to buzz around knocking against panes. Released at last, Priya lies as if crucified, his face buried in the sheet. It is the excruciating pain, now, nothing else, nothing else. He can barely move. The man pulls him to his feet with some impatience. His age demands that he rest. 'Take the chocolates or cigarettes,' he says carelessly. Priya does not realise that he is dismissed. He sways weakly and stares at nothing. Nothing registers. 'Get out,' the man orders impatiently, wanting to be alone. He lies back in the bed. He is filled with a sudden distaste for this brown thin child and for the sweat and fish smell that emanates from his body. He kicks Priya's shorts from the bed to the floor. Suddenly activated, Priya picks them up and draws them on. He whines with the slightest move.

He limps up to the table. He picks up a chocolate. His actions are hesitant. He opens the door and is about to creep out. The glare outside hits his eyes and his world swings back into focus. There is again sound and sense. The crash of waves, the stomach's gnaw, and the ache of Maya. He glances back at the man and sees his eyes closed. He sneaks back to the table. He crams his pockets with chocolates, chocolates, chocolates. He hurriedly grabs two of the oranges. 'The wrist watch,' he mumbles suddenly to the man in Sinhalese, his eyes on the watch. 'You said I could have the wrist watch.' The man fleetingly surfaces from twilight depths. 'Next week,' he murmurs, 'today – chocolates.'

I wait for Priya some distance away. He stops short and

glances at me fearfully. He would slink away. I hold out a few coins. His expression changes. He squares his frail shoulders and smiles a crooked smile.

He is in business.

WHAT ARE THE ROOTS THAT CLUTCH

MATTHEW KARPIN

Ahead of me, by perhaps three strokes, was her figure, balanced on the edge, in a bathing costume. One more stroke, and I ruptured the surface with a deliberate splash.

'Nicolo!' cried Wendy, now a little wet, and echoed by my wife Sarah, from one corner. Wiping my eyes, I was in time to see the water still dripping from her hair, but at the same time Craig Carrick in speedos, long legged and angular, approached the diving-ramp and leapt, cleanly slicing into the water over my head. His impact propelled backwash into my face.

'You won't stop him now,' said Wendy, and indeed, he had gained the opposite end very quickly and was heading back, directly to the point where I hung on. When he touched the edge and somersaulted, I followed down the pool with him, and for a lap, we swam side by side, stroke for stroke. After the turn at the other end, however, he pulled away strongly and reached Wendy well in advance of me. Gliding towards her, I drew myself out of the water, and sat puffing, as Craig continued to swim down his lane, graceful and quick.

'He's a good swimmer,' I admitted.

'Yes,' said Wendy dubiously, and Sarah, in her bikini, moved up and sat next to us.

The swimming pool, a mass of fluidity, reinvents everything it contains. I looked at the partially submerged body of Craig, distorted by refraction.

Craig reached our end of the pool again and splashlessly somersaulted into another lap.

Sarah commented ironically, 'He's quite a man, your man.'

'He's not who he thinks he is,' said Wendy.

However, he's in the running, I thought. His physical prowess, torso, tonicity, my Jewish body, short legs, mental agility. Various other characters with whom we would soon be sharing the pool began to appear on the margins in their differing states of undress. Soon two or three of these conference luminaries had dived in and joined Craig in performing laps until, sitting between the two girls, I had to watch the fierce but unannounced competition, power exuding through the fluid. A moment later, Craig came to our end again and unwedged himself from the water. He snatched his towel and sat between Wendy and me.

He looked at me glancingly, sideways, trying to read.

'There's nothing like it,' he said.

'There is,' I replied.

'Those bastards,' flicking his eyes back at the swimming pool, 'couldn't keep to their bloody lanes. It's more than just swimming in a straight line. Probably reflects their politics, as we may well see during the proceedings.'

I showed no signs of amusement. What does the man respond to?

I said, 'Possibly you require a swimming pool all to yourself. What kind of a line do you expect them to swim?'

Wendy stood up, the beautiful legs stretching out from behind him, her measured pace towards Sarah. The two young women walked behind us and away to an umbrella table.

'Unless you've been a competition swimmer, you don't understand. For years when I was growing up I had to use our local council pool to train and put up with the ignorance of the general public.'

Now he looked at me directly, but I continued to stare into the middle distance, unaware of his gaze.

He thinks it is his struggle, the disadvantage is his, he was not born into the mass culture, is separate, purer, the white boy, will not transpose himself.

'Well,' I said standing up to join the girls, 'all that splashing about is pretty much a waste of time.'

When I stood up in modest trunks to locate the girls, I realised that the entire conference resort had in the meantime filled up with people, mostly forming auricular groups of two or three, that speeches must have concluded. I left Craig without saying anything, and approached Wendy and Sarah, both looking at me as I came. Again Wendy stood up, saying, 'I'd better go back and find Craig.'

'You haven't been fighting with him, have you?' Sarah asked as I sat down.

I laughed and told her no, but my eyes traced Wendy's walk back. Lithely, she was at the pool and it appeared she might dive in. The variety of forms of substance, flesh in fluid, her limbs displacing air, the jump, displacing water.

'He is an arsehole, I grant you,' said Sarah.

Flesh will not always be as such, in earth, after death, in *articulo mortis, functus officio*, it loses its coherence, the beautiful girl, and all her consciousness, returned to the common pool. She broke the surface regularly, stroke by stroke, free-style, elastic, it reconstituted behind her, we pay the price for our intense particularity.

'I think Wendy is very nice, though. I'm sorry she's with him.'

'I agree,' I replied. 'I'm hoping she'll come to her senses, but there's no accounting.'

I looked up again. Craig was approaching in a strut, his dick-stickers giving him any prominence he had, and was evidently about to speak.

'I'm going back to our room,' he said, 'to change. I've done my laps.'

'Very good,' I replied.

Sarah said, looking at me for confirmation, 'I'll come with you Craig. I want to change into my clothes too.'

My wife gone, it left the field to me. Was she aware? Since the swimming pool had become so crowded, it took me a moment or two to re-locate Wendy, soon discovered to be back in the deep end, a good swimmer herself. I saw her face, turned, drawing air, the tops of her buttocks, the length of her legs. She glanced at me after a while as she trod water and saw I was alone.

I began to pull on my top, slowly, and wiped my eyes with my towel until, withdrawing it, I realised she was approaching. Soon she sat down at the umbrella table without saying anything and, knowing we were reasonably safe, I quickly brushed my lips on hers. That wetness is the context of life, the passing of my apprehension to you.

'Hello beautiful,' I said.

'Hello. How has the conference been going, do you think? How has Craig been?'

'He's somewhat unbearable, you know. I still have to find some mental space to figure out what I'm going to say in my speech.'

'You'll have no trouble, I think. He wants to take the "back to basics" line so you'll be able to depict him as conservative and out of touch.'

A moment, during which I thought it was unbearable that our relationship was secret, passed when I considered my animus, bringing me to this point, the need to outmanoeuvre, deceive, the necessity for unhappiness, stronger even than my desire for Wendy.

'We'd better not sit together for too long,' she said. 'He still thinks I dislike you. And there are plenty of people here who will talk to him.'

'No one like that I can see,' I said.

We both got up and headed towards the rooms. I let her go in front. Walking back, I was greeted enthusiastically by a number of delegates. *What branches grow*, the ability to unite people, to be known has replaced the need to know.

After lunch, which was a barbecue again bringing many of the delegates at the conference together, Sarah and I took a drive away from the beach town along the coast. The sun was brilliant and the swell far out into the ocean seemed to turn at the same rate as my change in ideas, while the noise of the tyres on the asphalt marked an infinity of divided emotions.

'When I spoke to Craig he seemed to be professing admiration for you,' Sarah finally said.

'How's that?' I asked.

'He made mention of your skill at speech-making. I think he's pretty nervous about having to stand up.'

'I can understand that.'

'He seems to think that the minds of the delegates are already made up as far as policy is concerned.'

'It sounds to me,' I said, 'as if he was trying to get you to tell him what I think. I hope you didn't say anything.'

'I didn't say anything.'

After a while, we drove beside a deserted beach and Sarah said, 'Let's get out here and have a swim.'

Having changed quickly on the sand, I was in first. I stood face on to the endless march of the waves and was surprised, when hit, by their strength. Sarah came in beside me. I dived under, green and white turbidity, and towards Sarah's legs, but already another wave had formed and lifted me off target. Accelerated change, to change back, re-constitution, human nature. Delegates, we have to determine what we can achieve, *realpolitik*.

'God!' Sarah said after a minute. 'It's so rough and there's no one else around. I think we should get out.'

Back in the car, we drove some more distance along the coast so that we could get back late and I wouldn't have to confront any more delegates that day. After an hour we turned around and had dinner at a restaurant we had seen, arriving back at our room in the evening. In bed, the motion which had been started continued. Sarah was on top of me, but I thought of Wendy's body, floating, *point d'appui*, and then, as I drifted into sleep, of fluidity.

In the morning I sat down at the desk in the room, while Sarah continued to sleep, in order to make more notes for my speech. There are clear choices, and the party is beginning to face them. The necessity to cajole without publicly admitting inadequacies. Particularly, on the question of immigration, we have to be expansive. We can choose more of the same, be monotonous, stagnant, or we can be open and hybrid. I would speak after Craig Carrick, the speech crucial in our preselection contest.

After half an hour and the completion of several pages of notes hastily scribbled, Sarah woke and left bed for her shower. Calling from the *en suite* as she dried herself she said, 'Do we have to attend the breakfast?'

'We're more or less obliged.'

'You'll be confronted by all the delegates you don't want to see.'

'I've mostly managed to avoid them so far but now I suppose I'll have to talk to them. That will be for a relatively short period before the conference starts again and I give my speech.'

Both dressed, we left our room and walked a short distance down the brick path to the breakfast room, opening the glass door, and there, across the room, was Wendy, with Craig Carrick. Moments later she saw me, the conjunction of eyes over the distance, the intervention only of air. What is possible is dependent partly on old decisions, which have locked us in, so that we are excluded from choice.

'Where do we sit?' asked Sarah.

Before I could decide, an assertive young man had called me, 'Nicolo, I'd like you to come and sit here, there's a space at our table for you and Sarah,' and as we sat, glancing across again, I saw her disappointment.

The young man asked, 'What are your feelings so far about the conference?'

Eating breakfast, adopting the manner of the celebrity, I replied, 'Well, I haven't so far had the chance to hear too many speeches.' The appropriate distance. 'But our over-riding concern will have to be to send a broad signal.' The young man stopped eating and listened; I continued. A number of tables seemed preoccupied with items on the agenda, while my own table of eight all listened carefully. Wendy's across the room was also connected to mine. The waves that connect us and then pull us apart. We are in our element, the empirical world, but we will never be permanently united. For all our plans we will remain elemental and parallel. I saw her eyes again. Craig at her table was sounding forth and had his adherents.

After a while, however, he stood up from his table, and headed towards me; Wendy came behind him.

'Starting soon, Nicolo,' he said on gaining my breakfast group, interrupting the young man who had been telling me something. 'It will be pretty lively, no doubt.'

How very true, old sport. Always the first to make the move.

For a moment or two I said nothing. Finally I answered, 'No question about it,' after briefly raising my head to look at Carrick, and quickly turned back to the young man.

Craig walked away. I did not look at Wendy. The young man stopped talking as Sarah and I finished breakfast. It would soon be time to move into the conference room.

'I'm a little upset for Wendy,' Sarah said.

We looked across at their table where Carrick was shaking someone's hand and Wendy stood as if dejected. I caught her eye but she looked suddenly away when she realised Sarah was also gazing. That stretch of space which flowed between us joining and separating us, the visual transmission of shared humanity.

I stood up.

'We'd really better go in now, Sarah; I think I'll have to talk to the chair of the panel before it starts.'

I shook hands with everyone at my breakfast table and continued to greet delegates and others as we walked to the conference room. Inside the room, already containing many people, Sarah took a seat in the audience, finding Wendy, and I moved up to the front. Four others, including Carrick, sat in chairs on the rostrum.

There was a little introduction by the chair and one delegate began to speak on the question of the party's inclusiveness. As he spoke, my glance was at Wendy and Sarah, alliances which are fashioned in ignorance, we don't tolerate disloyalty, cannot include those who betray us. Carrick then spoke for some minutes. He said he believed delegates were generally aware of where he stood on such questions and that his recent legal representation of a group of boat people had received some coverage. We must be a more inclusive society, he said, and received applause.

The applause stirred through the audience, the concentric, the ripple of influence, my girls applauded politely.

When I spoke, last, I said it was important not to deceive ourselves. We had to know whom to deceive. There was some laughter, and in particular, from Wendy. We could marginalise ourselves with fairy stories, or empower ourselves. Oceans hold us apart, oceans join us. 'Delegates, we have to determine what we can achieve. It is a matter of *realpolitik*.'

My win.

The business part of the conference was over and now I could take time off. The weather was still fine. It seemed most likely that in the afternoon I would find Wendy at the swimming pool.

After winding up with conversations and some photographs, I headed towards Sarah.

She said, 'It was excellent.'

'I more or less called him a liar,' I said.

'Yes, but an incompetent one.'

Avoiding people who began to approach, I walked with Sarah briskly to the exit. Outside milling groups of the audience allowed me through and Sarah and I discussed the rest of the day before the flight home in the evening. She would shop while I would simply relax.

In half an hour she took the car and, in my bathers,

if my understanding was correct, I could cross that space, emptiness, again for a snatched hour. If she shared my ruse. The pool, I discovered, was occupied by two or three swimmers, in leisurely mode. What was real in the atmosphere of the conference room is not in this jelly. Firstly, it bends the light, refraction. Secondly, our motion through water is as if retarded.

I sat at the edge, with my head lowered, when I was splashed by a diver. Looking up, I saw that it was Wendy.

'Hello, Nicolo,' she said, treading water.

'I was hoping I'd see you here.'

She did a somersault and her bottom was displayed, before she came out and sat beside me.

'Craig's gone,' she said, as she towelled her face. 'Your speech was very good and he's quite upset about it.'

'Yes, I imagine,' I replied.

'He took your reference to deception personally. But I think it's served its purpose and you'll win preselection over him.'

There was still some doubt, but I would not discuss it with her. One of the swimmers floated past us.

I asked, 'How are you coping with Craig yourself?'

'He is actually good company for me most of the time. I would rather it were different, I'd rather your company. He thinks I talk with Sarah because she sat with me, and he wanted me to find out what I could, which is what he thinks I am doing now.'

When we returned to the room she had shared with Craig, Wendy said, 'I'd like you to think about leaving Sarah.'

I told her, 'I have been.'

Kissing, at last, the unbearable space removed, the necessity for deception remained.

A TASTE FOR IT

MONICA McINERNEY

Maura picked up her wineglass and spoke in a low, sexy voice. 'I'm rich and full-bodied and you'll savour my taste for a long, long time.'

'It's a wine label, not *Playboy* magazine,' her brother Nick said under his breath, not looking up from his writing-pad.

Maura took another sip of red wine and tried again. 'What about "fruitier than Carmen Miranda's hat and a lot easier to carry"?'

Nick didn't even smile. 'Maura, you're not taking this seriously, are you?' He ripped out another page of scribbled notes from his writing-pad and threw it onto the growing pile on the floor.

She *had* been taking the label-writing seriously. For the first four days anyway. But they were now into day five of the process and she was rapidly running out of adjectives.

They went through this several times a year, when the various blends Nick made in their small winery were ready for bottling. Nick was usually very easy-going, but he fell into a high anxiety state when it came to his labels. He was convinced the perfect combination of words hinting at full flavours and bursting taste sensations produced extra sales.

Maura softened as she looked at her brother's worried expression. 'Nick, your wine is so good, it doesn't matter what's written on the label. Let's just tell it like it is. "Here's a fantastic Shiraz. It was made in South Australia. We hope you enjoy it."'

'No, far too straightforward. This is the wine industry, remember?' He looked up at her with a glimmer of a grin. 'Besides, I want it to be extravagant. There are three years of my life in those bottles.'

There was silence again as they both went back over their notes. Maura surreptitiously checked her watch. She had half an hour before she had to start preparing for today's lunch crowd. She picked up her glass again, letting the morning sunlight stream through the deep red wine.

'What about "ruby rich in flavour, colour and appeal, a gem among Clare Valley reds"?'

'Now, that's more like it.' Nick actually smiled, scribbling down her suggestion.

The sudden peal of the telephone made them both jump.

Maura got to it first. 'Lorikeet Hill Winery Café, good morning.' Her voice warmed. 'Joel, hello! How are you?' Nick looked up as Maura walked out into the garden with the portable phone. That would be the last he'd see of her for a while, if her usual conversations with Joel were any guide. Maura and Joel had become friends when she had lived in Sydney, where Joel worked as a freelance food writer. He moved from office to office, usually finding time to ring Maura for a good long catch-up at some editor's expense.

Nick was surprised when she came back into the reception area less than five minutes later, a mischievous smile on her face.

'I've got some news,' she said.

That was no shock. Joel was the gossip king of the food world. Nick waited.

'The Diner, the *OzTaste* magazine food critic, is coming here today.'

'What! *The Diner!* How on earth does Joel know that?'

Maura sat down. 'He was calling from the *OzTaste* office. He just happened to see a confidential list of the critic's restaurant visits this month. And he just happened to read it closely and notice we're the lucky one for today. Apparently The Diner's travelling around the country with his wife reviewing regional restaurants.'

Nick looked worried. 'That's really bad news, isn't it? Isn't he the one that closed down Gemma's restaurant?'

Maura nodded. Several years previously her friend Gemma had opened a small bistro in Sydney. All had gone well until The Diner had visited and written a vicious – and factually incorrect – review. Overnight it had destroyed her trade. Gemma had demanded an apology from the editor, and had received a well-hidden two-line retraction in the next issue. But the damage had been done. The customers had stayed away in droves.

'Did Joel have any good news?' Nick asked.

Maura smiled broadly. 'Today's review will never be published. *OzTaste* magazine is closing down. Joel's heard the publisher's been taken over by some international magazine group and there's going to be a big change in direction. But it's still hush-hush and The Diner wouldn't have heard the news yet.'

'So he'll soon be out of a job?'

'Just like Gemma was when he closed her restaurant.'

They were silent for a moment.

'If this is going to be his last free meal, we really should make sure it's one to remember, shouldn't we?' Maura said thoughtfully.

'Make sure he never forgets us, do you mean?'

'Pull out all the stops,' she grinned.

As her kitchen and waiting staff began to arrive, Maura took great pleasure in explaining the situation, promising a fifty-dollar bonus for the most inventive revenge tactics.

Her head waiter Rob was especially taken with the idea. 'He's an arrogant pig, apparently,' he said with feeling. 'He made a waitress friend of mine in Melbourne cry once, he was so rude to her. Leave him to me.'

In the kitchen, Maura cast an eye over the list of dishes her other customers would be choosing from: a warm garlic, herb and mushroom salad, made with herbs from the Lorikeet Hill garden; a Thai-style beef salad with mint, coriander and peanuts; grilled lamb cutlets with potato and parsnip mash; tangy yoghurt chicken with roasted capsicum and garlic; and a zesty fruit sorbet served with poached nectarines. The dessert was one of her favourites, and was always a hit with the customers. Ironically, she had adapted it from a recipe she had found in an old issue of *OzTaste*.

Thinking of the magazine, she suddenly recalled an article The Diner had written a year or so back, in which he'd included a list of his dining-out pet hates. She and Gemma had laughed about it, wondering how the editor had kept the list to one page. With an idea hatching, she hunted for the issue in the box of magazines she kept as reference.

There it was. Maura frowned as she read his article again. It was people like him who gave food writing a bad name, she thought, as she skimmed through the pompous introduction to his article.

Australian food has certainly come on somewhat in recent years, but far too many times I have had the misfortune of being served food better suited to seventies dinner parties or countrywomen's association annual dinners, invariably delivered by drop-outs from a second-rate catering college.

Maura quickly scanned his list of pet hates. Perfect. She'd be able to manage them all easily. She'd get her waiter Rob to explain to the critic that they were trialling a new style of dining. They'd serve him a number of small dishes, in a Lorikeet Hill version of the famous Spanish tapas style. It would work a treat.

By 1.30 pm the café was about three-quarters full of a mixture of local people and visitors from Adelaide, up for a day of fine Clare Valley food and wine. Out in the reception area, Maura smiled goodbye as a couple left, carrying half a dozen of the newly released Lorikeet Hill Cabernet Sauvignon.

Maura mused for a moment, wondering where that wine would be when it was opened. She loved the whole winemaking process. Lorikeet Hill was right in the middle of the vineyards of the Clare Valley, one of the most beautiful parts of South Australia, and she saw the vines through all the seasons, from the bare branches of winter, to the sudden blast of light green in the spring. She liked to imagine the whole process as a fast-forward film – the grapes flourishing, swelling from tiny seeds to plump ovals on the vines, the early morning sight of groups of grape-pickers, moving down the long, long rows, like flocks of birds eating all the fruit . . .

The noise of a car engine outside caught her attention. Looking out from the reception window she watched a car with interstate number plates manoeuvre into the small carpark. This had to be him.

She watched as the passengers took great pains to engage the car alarm and carefully lock the doors. Just as well, Maura thought. The possums around here were notorious car thieves.

She caught a glimpse as a couple made their way up the tree-lined path. A tall, dark-haired man, with an equally tall, very slender young woman beside him. Her hair was styled in a stark, angular bob and she was wearing a close-fitting bright-pink dress. As for the King of Critics – he was hardly the stooped, overweight, gout-ridden elderly gentleman they'd been expecting, Maura thought in surprise. He didn't even look forty. Thirty-five maybe. At least six foot tall, she judged, watching as he ducked under the garden arch. Dark, maybe even black hair. And from this distance his physique looked more like that of an athlete on his day off than a man who ate for a living.

Moments later the doorbell jangled as the couple walked in. Maura nearly laughed aloud – the man was carrying a copy of *OzTaste*'s guide to regional restaurants. Well, that was subtle. She'd heard of some critics who insisted on anonymity. This one was obviously the opposite, dropping hints so he'd get the best treatment.

She took a moment to look at him closely, taking advantage as their eyesight adjusted to the dim, cool light of the reception area. She nearly wolf-whistled. He was gorgeous.

Beautifully dressed in a white linen shirt and close-fitting dark jeans. Tanned, lean feature, yet his face looked lived-in, not male-model smooth. He and his girlfriend looked like they had just stepped off the set of an expensive aftershave commercial.

It wasn't fair, she thought, suddenly feeling a rush of dislike for him. Not only did he make his living wreaking havoc on poor restaurateurs like Gemma, but by the looks of things he lived a glamorous, charmed life as well. Maura thought cheerfully of the imminent closure of *OzTaste*. A taste of his own medicine at last.

Still, Maura decided on one last check before it was all systems go with what they had dubbed 'Gemma's Revenge'. Heaven knows she didn't want a poor innocent couple from Adelaide to go through this particular experience. Joel had been unable to give her a detailed description of The Diner but had alerted her to his distinctive voice. 'He grew up in New York,' Joel had hurriedly explained on the phone that morning, 'and he's still got traces of an American accent, even after years here in Sydney. I've heard him being interviewed on the radio. But I'm sure he'll stand out – by all accounts he's not the easiest of customers.'

He was right. These two stood out like sore thumbs.

She decided on two quick tests – if she managed to hear his American accent and find out they'd driven from Sydney, then it was full steam ahead.

'Good afternoon,' she said brightly. 'Welcome to Lorikeet Hill – can I help you?'

The stylish woman answered in a drawling voice. 'Yes, we'd like some lunch – I sure hope we're not too late.'

'Oh, there's no such thing as time in the country,' Maura answered lightly. 'Have you driven a long way?'

The man answered, in a deep, almost musical voice. 'We've come from Sydney, but we've broken the trip over a few days.' Maura strained to catch his accent, but he'd spoken too low to be sure. But they'd come from Sydney . . .

'Sydney?' Maura repeated, almost shouting. 'How lovely! Well, you're both very welcome to the Clare Valley and Lorikeet Hill. Your table will be ready in just a moment. But could I just ask you both, if I may be so bold, are those American accents I hear?'

'Yes, I'm from New York,' the woman replied, in a bored tone of voice.

'And you, sir?' Maura pressed.

'I lived there for a number of years,' he answered,

looking a little puzzled at the sudden interest in accents.

'Ah, America, land of the free – and you've just driven down from Sydney, well, that's terrific!' Maura felt her voice get slightly high-pitched. 'Just one moment please and I'll have someone escort you to your table.'

'Have someone escort you to your table?' What had come over her? She'd never said that in all her years in restaurants. She walked quickly back into the kitchen, where her staff waited.

Maura gave a big wink. 'Thank you, Rob – if you could please show our most honoured guests to their table.'

'My pleasure, Miss Carmody,' Rob said with a wide smile.

The staff peered around the kitchen door to watch.

The sleek woman was checking her reflection in the glass-framed photographs by the door, while the critic was reading the food and wine reviews pinned to a noticeboard on the wall.

Rob coughed politely, and as they turned around, greeted them with a shocking grimace, far removed from his usual sweet smile. Maura watched as the couple tried not to react. 'Bon jour, madam and mizure, pliz follow me to ze table we 'ave chosen for you,' Rob said, adopting an appalling stage-French accent.

Rob was a born actor, Maura thought. He chattered away as he led the couple through the entire café, weaving in and out of every table in the dining-room, before returning to the first table they had passed on their tour. 'Sit 'ere, pliz. I 'ope you enjoy ze special taste sensations we 'ave prepared for you today. Zee wine waitress, she will be wiz you shortly.' With a flamboyant bow, he placed their napkins on their knees and flounced off.

Pet hate one – fussy, fake French waiters – done, Maura thought to herself. She came out to the reception desk again and eavesdropped as the couple settled into their seats.

'What on earth's going on here? This isn't a French restaurant, is it?' she heard the woman hiss.

'It's supposed to be modern Australian,' the man replied, checking the *OzTaste* guide. 'But didn't that waiter say something about the Spanish tapas style?'

'Well, by the look of these decorations it's more like a fake Irish pub,' the woman sniffed. 'We'll have tin whistles playing jigs and reels next.'

'Thanks for the idea,' Maura whispered to herself. Fake Irish, indeed. The white walls of the café were decorated with the originals of a series of beautiful paintings Fran, Nick's wife, had done for their wine labels. Depicting musicians and Irish scenes, the paintings reflected the Irish heritage of the Clare Valley.

Maura moved over to the compact disc player and lowered the volume on the classical CD playing. 'The lady in pink over there has just told me she's Irish and very homesick and I just want to play her some music to cheer her up,' she explained to one of the larger groups.

The customers nodded and smiled – *Riverdance* had done wonders for the popularity of Irish music and they had all been lulled by the fine Lorikeet Hill food and wine.

Maura found a CD called *Tin Whistle Favourites for All the Family* that Nick had given to her as a joke the year before. The shrill sound of the whistle began to fill the café, concentrated on the table in the corner. How unfortunate that Mr and Mrs Critic have been seated there, Maura thought, as she moved the volume control higher and higher.

The other guests tapped their toes as the squawking increased. The guests of honour moved angrily in their seats, trying to get a staff member's attention and shouting over the music to make themselves heard.

Turning down the music to a dull squeal, Maura mentally reviewed the hit-list again. Pet hate two, loud background music. Two down, four to go, she thought with pleasure. With a wink, she sent her star wine waiter Annie into the fray.

For someone who had just graduated top of the class from a wine appreciation course, Annie did a terrific job of pretending to be completely ignorant about all the wine. She deliberately misheard every question either of the two asked her. She spoke about Riesling as though it was made from Shiraz grapes. And to top it off she made sure she was clearly visible as she filled their glasses from a cheap cask of mass-produced wine Rob had rushed out and bought that morning.

'Number three done with perfection, Annie,' Maura whispered. Now, time for the food.

Rob delivered their first course with great pomp and ceremony – two huge platters of deep-fried canned asparagus spears coated in breadcrumbs. The dish would have looked perfectly at home on the cover of a seventies cookbook. The can of polyunsaturated oil she had used certainly delivered the critic's pet hate number four too – several times over.

Back in the kitchen, Maura put the finishing touches to their next course – chicken à la paprika. But Maura felt her hand accidentally slip as she was adding more of the spice. Now it was more paprika à la chicken. And a bit of fresh chilli always went a very long way, she thought, adding three teaspoons of freshly cut red chilli, seeds and all. Number five – tick, she thought gleefully.

Having removed the untouched asparagus Rob delivered the chicken dish to their table with great pizzazz, placing the plates in front of them with dramatic flourishes, *voilà*s, hooplas and every other vaguely French-sounding word he could remember. Maura and the kitchen staff waited as the couple took their first mouthful.

The spluttering began in seconds. She heard their coughing from inside the kitchen, and peeped through the glass doors leading into the dining-room in time to see the woman grasp the napkin to her mouth and make a dash for the bathroom.

Maura took the chance to beard the lion in his den. The critic seemed to be suffering a silent coughing attack, his eyes streaming, his voice hoarse as he tried to say something.

'Oh, I am sorry,' Maura said in a saccharine-sweet voice, as she walked over to his table. 'Was that a little too spicy for your delicate palate? How awful! And I understand your sixth pet hate is having to ask for water in restaurants. Here, let me save you the trouble.'

She actually hadn't planned her final action. But a

memory-flash of the trouble he had caused Gemma suddenly made her see red.

Almost in slow motion, she picked up the large vase of flowers standing on the cupboard beside her, took out the flowers and poured the cold liquid slowly over his head.

'It comes with Gemma Taylor's compliments,' she added for good measure, deciding it was time to come clean.

The only sound he made was a deep gasp, but that was enough to attract the attention of the other customers. They began to whisper and giggle at the sight of the man dripping water, with Maura standing beside him, vase in hand.

She had to admire his coolness, but really, with a back full of water she could hardly expect anything else. He gave her a long slow look.

Maura had intended to give him a passionate lecture on the importance of getting his facts right and the severe effects his reviews could have. But a shriek from his companion as she flounced back to their table stole the moment. She took a breath as though she was about to begin shouting when the man laid a hand on her arm.

'Thank you, Carla, but I don't think there's anything you can add to this very strange situation. Are you ready to leave?' The man rose from his seat, giving his head a slight shake, which only spread the water further. 'I had hoped after the asparagus and paprika that this meal couldn't possibly get any worse, but now I wouldn't like to bet on it.'

'Well, we're certainly not paying for that garbage!' the young woman almost spat at Maura. 'This is the most appalling restaurant I have ever been in.' She strode to the door. 'You should be reported!' she shouted over her shoulder as they made a noisy exit.

Rob and Annie hurried out of the kitchen, congratulating each other.

'Gemma would have loved it,' Nick said, still laughing. 'Revenge accomplished. We should have hired a video camera.'

Maura smiled with them, but didn't feel as elated as she had hoped. There was something in the man's gaze which had unsettled her. She mentally shook herself. It was just the surprise of him being attractive, when you were expecting an overweight old boor, she told herself. You've been out in the sticks too long – you're not used to handsome, sophisticated men.

As she heard the front door open again, Maura went out to greet the new arrivals. She tried to ignore the sight of Rob giving a reprise of his French waiter's act, with his fifty-dollar bonus clenched between his teeth. The kitchen assistants were in hysterics.

The newcomers, an elderly couple, looked over in a puzzled manner at this noise.

'You all seem very happy today,' the man said in a slightly drawn-out, disapproving voice.

'Oh, I think it's the country air,' Maura explained as she led them to the newly reset table. 'Now, can I show you the menu?'

THE KISS

PETER GOLDSWORTHY

The thunder is closer now, almost seismic, as much inside the car as outside. 'Just made it,' Kenny says.

He noses the dusty Mercedes in among the pillars that support the house, and switches off the ignition and lights. Utter darkness.

'Relax,' Tom says somewhere in that darkness. 'The car would have dried overnight.'

His voice, as disembodied as the thunder, seems to have Kenny surrounded.

'Yeah – streaked like a fucking zebra.'

'You worry too much. Live a little, for Christ's sake.'

His friend is right, Kenny knows. They could have joyridden the dusty back roads till dawn and still had time to clean the car; his parents are not due back till late the next day. 'It's my neck,' he says. 'Not yours.'

Tom isn't listening. 'Take the old zebra for another

gallop,' he mutters somewhere, and chuckles again, pleased with himself. 'Take the old zebra back out on the savannah ... '

'Just empty the fucking ashtray before you get out,' Kenny says.

There is no anger in his words; the obscenity comes as naturally as music, a necessary rhythm.

'Say please.'

'Just do it.'

He climbs from the car and walks out from beneath the house into the October light-and-sound show. The humid weight of the impending Wet presses down upon him, squeezing an answering wetness, a kind of juice, from his skin, but he is beyond the discomforts of heat and sweat. The dark night air carries powerful scents: a cusp-mix of Wet season and Dry, dust and imminent rain. The thunder is constant, a rumbling sound horizon. Lightning flashbulbs the darkness, alternating night and day. The first rains are surely no more than hours away, although they have seemed no more than hours away for weeks. Tom's voice, at his shoulder, startles him. 'Drink?'

The sherry flagon is offered; Kenny waves it away. Tom takes a swig before speaking again.

'This is just a tease,' he says. 'Foreplay. The Wet is still a week away.'

'Bullshit. It's going to piss down any second.'

Mention of the various liquids – rain, sherry, piss – seems to increase the pressure in Kenny's bladder. He vaults the low back-fence, and walks to the edge of the small cliff above the beach. Lightning flickers with special intensity on the far side of the harbour, a distant fireworks, embedded in banked cloud. Perhaps the Dry has already ended over there. More lightning; the mud-flats below are revealed, hidden, then revealed again, the low tide-line half a mile out. Tom materialises at his side; they unzip and send two long, steady arcs of urine over the edge of the cliff and down into the darkness of the mangroves. Years before it would have been a simple contest – higher, further; contests mostly won by Tom. At sixteen, sweet-and-sour sixteen, Kenny is finding words more useful weapons. 'It's a lightning conductor,' he says.

'What is?'

'Piss, stupid.'

The idea strikes them as hilarious; they laugh convulsively, their streams becoming broken, scattering showers.

Tom leans back and aims his cock near-vertically: 'Way to go!'

The dare is unpunished by the heavens. Kenny vaults back over the fence, grabs the garden hose, twists on the tap, and aims the gushing water at his friend.

'Mine is bigger than yours!'

'Longer, maybe.'

Tom, bigger and stronger, soon wrests the nozzle from him; the spray is turned back into his own face, point-blank. The coldness of the water – a deep earth-cold – gives only temporary reprieve from the sticky heat. They lie in soaked clothes, on wet grass, sweating. The night is dead calm; no air movement cools their skins. 'Sure you don't want a drink?' Tom's words remind Kenny there is work to be done, evidence to be disposed of. He pushes himself to his feet, walks back beneath the house and gropes inside the car between lightning flashes. The brandy bottle is still half-full, to be watered down and replaced in the liquor cabinet. The moulded glass bottle of sparkling wine – Pineapple Pearl – is empty; its absence from his parents' fridge still seems a gamble worth taking. He checks the ashtray. Of course it has not been emptied; he empties it himself. The picnic rug on the backseat is briefly illuminated. He tugs it through the open window, steps back onto the lawn, and shakes out the gritty beach sand over his wet, prostrate friend.

'Do you mind?' Tom says.

'What are you complaining about? You've been rolling around in the sand with Debbie all night.'

'Jealousy's a curse, Kenny.'

Is he jealous, Kenny wonders? If so, jealous of whom? Of Tom for beating him to the pleasures of Debbie, or of Debbie for intruding on a boys' night out?

Tom rambles drunkenly on, beyond nuances: 'I thought you were never going to leave us. I thought you were going to hang around and watch.'

'Who needed to watch? I could hear everything half a mile up the beach.'

'Wha's that supposed to mean?'

'The noise she was making. What were you doing to her?'

'How could she make any noise? Her mouth was full.'

Kenny almost chokes himself, with laughter; Tom can always make him laugh. He flings the rug into the air above his friend; it seems to hang there, a parachute canopy, momentarily suspended, floating on the viscid air, before settling.

'Fold that up. Please.' He strips off his wet shirt, slings it over the clothesline, then climbs the steps up into the house. The slatted metal louvres that form the outside walls of each room have been cranked wide-open, but no breeze yet enters. He switches the big overhead fan to maximum notch, the heavy air begins to stir. He is searching the fridge when Tom appears in the door with a roughly bundled picnic rug under his arm.

'Anything cold in the fridge?'

'Butter,' Kenny tells him. 'Eggs.'

'Very funny. Anything to drink?'

'Milk.'

Tom topples theatrically backwards onto the sofa, as if shot.

'What I need is a swim,' he announces.

The lightning flicker, on cue, might have been a warning sent from Kenny's parents.

'Swim in the bathtub,' he tells his friend. 'The car stays where it is.'

'We could break into the pool.'

'How do we get there? Transporter beam?'

Flopped on his back on the sofa, Tom takes another swig of sherry, thinking. 'The water tank? It's closer than the pool.'

'We'd still have to fucking drive there.'

Even as he speaks, the notion of a swim is growing on Kenny. Debbie has been dropped home not more than an hour past her curfew, the night is still young, its hours small and empty. The alcohol is leaching from his system, he is feeling restless again.

'We could ride,' he finally announces. 'If you can keep your bike upright.'

Sitting beneath the big, cooling fan, the task does not seem beyond them. Tom rises and follows him unsteadily down the steps. The pushbikes are leaning against a pillar beneath the house; they set off immediately, riding abreast, bare-chested, weaving and wobbling a little. The lightning has eased, but their sweating torsos glisten as they pass through the successive light-fields of the street-lamps. The night air is resistant to movement, hot and viscous, difficult to breathe; Tom, heavy with his own thick flesh, is soon struggling for air. The cooling breeze of their own motion fails to keep pace with the outpouring of sweat; soon Kenny, too, is up off his saddle, standing high on the pedals, pushing down as if riding uphill but getting nowhere fast, as if tethered to his starting point by invisible elastic.

At the top of the descent to the beach-flats they pause to take breath. Sporadic flashes of lightning illume the view. On the far side of the wide flats the road rises again to Bullocky Point. The huge tank and its reservoir of cooling water is still impossibly distant, perched high on the far point.

'Seemed like a good idea at the time,' Kenny says.

'Not one of your better ones.'

'It gets worse. We'll have to ride all the way back home afterwards.'

'So you don't want a swim?'

'Did I say that?'

A slow, drunken smile creases Tom's face: 'You're not fucking suggesting?'

Kenny answers by turning his bike back towards home. His friend hoots, loudly. 'I don't believe my ears. Half an hour ago you were shitting yourself about the car.'

'I'm older now.'

'You grow up quick.'

They ride home at speed, forcing themselves through the muggy air, knowing the tank is much closer now, even if they are pedalling in the opposite direction.

'Bring the sherry!' Tom shouts upstairs as Kenny fetches the car-keys, but he already has the flagon in hand, feeling reckless and ready for anything, as if overcoming his guilt about taking the car is the first step in a more general unravelling. The night is beginning again for the two of them, the old team, no outsiders. He backs out of the drive at speed, crashes through the gear-change, and accelerates away with a squeal of tyre-rubber. 'Petrol's low,' Tom notices.

The news seems only mildly alarming. At the top of the beach road Ken switches off the engine, and coasts in neutral down the long incline, windows wound down, the air moving sweetly across his upper body. Many times the boys have freewheeled down this same slope on their pushbikes, the contest to glide as far as possible without pedalling, slowing gradually once the beach flats are reached. Tom benefits from his extra-bulk; sometimes he can nurse his faltering bike as far as the Gardens. The heavy metal mass of the car carries them even further before Kenny restarts the engine for the last ascent. The big water tank looms out of the darkness on Bullocky Point, a squat, square concrete fortress, or gun emplacement. Kenny parks on the far side, hidden from the main road. Tom is first out of the car, stripping himself one-handed, the sherry flagon clutched in the other. He kicks himself free of shorts and thongs, and rapidly clambers the rusted metal ladder fixed to the northern wall of the tank, still wearing his jocks. As Kenny joins him at the top, he is draining the last of the sherry. They gaze down from a high ledge into the dark interior. No water level can be seen; the inside ladder descends into blackness.

Kenny feels a flicker of apprehension: 'Maybe it's empty.'

'Better toss something in,' Tom says, and grapples playfully with his friend, jostling him towards the edge.

'Fuck off.'

Tom releases him, and with a flip of his wrist tosses the empty flagon far out into the void.

The splash is invisible, but noisily resonant, amplified within the vast echo chamber.

'Last one in!'

'You don't know how deep it is!' Kenny shouts, but Tom has already launched himself out into nothingness.

This time the splash is visible, a brief silver explosion against a dark field, followed by the glimmer of spreading ripples catching and reflecting the weak light.

Tom's voice follows, echoing loudly within the four walls: 'Chicken!'

Kenny leaps immediately from the ledge, freefalling, it seems, for far too long. The sudden cold smack of the water is half reassuring, half shocking, stopping his heart, paralysing his breathing muscles. He surfaces, unable to breathe for a long moment. The walls and corners of the tank are as black as ink, but as his eyes accommodate he begins to sense the pale moon of a face somewhere in the centre, lit only by the faint glimmer of starlight and the cloud-reflected lights of the town. 'So – what did you do with Debbie?' he asks the moon-face.

'A gentleman never tells,' the face tells him.

They might be shouting, their voices are so amplified, reverberant. Kenny lowers his: 'What's being a gentleman got to do with you?'

Tom laughs as loudly as ever. 'I thought you said you could hear everything.'

'It didn't leave a lot to the imagination.'

'It was weird, Kenny. She let me do everything – except kiss her. Said I was too pissed.'

'I'd have to be pissed to kiss her.'

Tom ignores him: 'She told me a good story. She was kissing some guy at a party last year, and he suddenly stops, turns away to spew up over her shoulder, then goes right on kissing her.'

'Choice,' Kenny says, and kicks away, a few lazy backstrokes. When he turns back, his friend's face has vanished.

'Ribbit,' a frog croaks, a throaty basso in a dark corner. 'Ribbit.'

Kenny's tone is scornful: 'Five out of ten.'

A human voice answers: 'It wasn't me, fuckwit.'

'You expect me to believe there are frogs in here?'

'Where would you spend the Dry if you were a frog?'

'How would I get in? Hop from rung to rung?'

Tom's face materialises, pale grey on black, and they float in silence on their backs, side by side, for a time.

'Where is the ladder?' Tom asks.

'Had enough?'

'I'm feeling a bit wonky. I might throw up.'

'Don't expect a goodnight kiss.' Kenny peers up at the high rim of the tank, an ill-defined margin between the total blackness of the interior, and the star-pricked darkness of the night-sky. A first, slight shiver: he, too, has no idea which side the ladder is on.

'I'll feel around the edge.' He kicks himself to the nearest corner of the tank, finding it by touch, then sets off, side-stroke, trailing one hand along the slimy wall. A faint premonition of tiredness enters the muscles of his upper arms, a slight heaviness, or resistance to movement; after the second corner he rolls onto his back, and propels himself using his legs alone, long lazy frog-kicks.

'Where are you?' Tom's voice is some distance away, but loudly resonant, rebounding between walls. 'On the last wall. Can't find it.'

As he floats, resting, the obvious strikes him: 'It's the end of the Dry. The water level is below the bottom rung.'

'So what do we fucking do? Wait for the monsoon to float us up?'

They tread water in silence, listening. The thunder is no more than a distant grumble, a faint tremor in the water. Or is the tremor internal, another shiver? Kenny has earnt his Lifesaving Certificate years before, half rite-of-passage, half trial-by-ordeal. He feels at home in the water – but the weary ache in his upper arms is growing. 'I'm not feeling good about this,' Tom is saying somewhere.

'We'll be fine. Just float till daybreak.'

'Then what? No-one will find us.'

'We can yell.'

Silence, then Tom again: 'I am going to throw up.'

'Hold onto it, for Christ's sake.'

The noise of retching is close at hand.

'Choice,' Kenny mutters, and kicks away into the middle of the tank. 'Fucking choice.' Lying on his back, half-sunk in the huge mattress of water, he scrutinises the tops of the walls. Shreds of cloud move slowly across the starry square of the night-sky, as if on some darkened movie screen. 'You okay?'

Tom seems to spit his answer out, as if the words are the last vestige of vomit: 'Fucking wonderful.'

Kenny floats on, trying to keep calm, to think things through, but Tom won't leave him alone: 'How did we get into this fucking mess?'

'You jumped, remember?'

'You didn't fucking stop me!'

'So it's my fault?' Silence in the great vault, till a thought strikes Kenny: 'Which side is the ladder on?'

'The school side.'

He feels a stirring of anger towards his friend: 'I know that, dickhead. Which side? North?'

'Northwest.'

'Then the ladder is on the far wall. The weather is coming from the northwest.'

'So?'

'Maybe I can give you a leg up. Try and grab it.'

'Grab something I can't even see?'

'You got any better ideas?' Kenny kicks across the tank to the northern wall, then side-strokes slowly from one corner to the other, measuring the length of the wall in hand-spans, counting each aloud. 'What the fuck are you doing?'

'Shut up – now I have to start again.'

Tom keeps his mouth shut, compliant for the first time that night, perhaps for the first time in all their years of friendship. Reaching the end of the wall, a hundred and seventy-two spans, Kenny counts back half that number and scratches a shallow groove into the thin rind of slime above the water level.

'What if the ladder's off-centre?' Tom asks.

'Just get over here.'

Kenny treads water below the imagined ladder, willing it to be there. He clasps ten fingers together to form a foothold, Tom plants his right foot into this makeshift stirrup and heaves himself up. The weight submerges Kenny completely; he surfaces to find Tom a few feet out, breathing hard.

'Nothing there.'

'Two steps this time – one onto my hands, then up onto my shoulders.' The force of the recoil submerges him again, more deeply; after gaining his breath, they try again. 'We're doing this the wrong way around. I should be on top.'

He launches himself upwards from Tom's clasped hands, his own hands finding nothing in the darkness but the dry, crusted wall. Tom's panicky voice is echoing through the chamber as Kenny surfaces after the fifth or sixth such attempt. 'I've got a cramp.'

Kenny is hit in the face by a flailing arm.

'Kenny? Give us a hand. I need to hold onto something.'

'Lie on your back,' he says. 'All you have to do is float.'

Tom rolls onto his back, but almost immediately rolls back again.

'Jesus – now the other one is seizing up. All that fucking jumping.'

'Float on your back. I'll stretch your legs.'

But Tom is grasping at him again, frantic: 'Just let me hold on for a minute.'

The weight of his bigger friend submerges Kenny; he kicks free underwater, on the edge of panic himself. 'Where are you?' Tom is shouting as he breaks surface. 'Kenny? Where are you?'

'Keeping my distance unless you do what I fucking say.' This time the words sink in. Kenny supports Tom with one hand beneath the chin, keeping the mouth and nose just above the surface. He has to work harder himself, treading water at jogging pace, and knows he cannot continue indefinitely, but Tom is in some pain. Breathing heavily, his words come in gasps.

'Jesus, Kenny – what are we going to do?'

The question shocks Kenny; it seems too general, too open-ended. Far better to stick to particulars. 'Panic makes cramp worse. It'll ease if you stretch the legs.'

'It's not easing.'

'It will. Try to ignore it.'

His mind gropes for solutions. He tries to remember the Lifesaving lessons, three long years before. Half the battle is mental – is that what he had been taught?

'You know,' he says in Tom's ear, 'you still haven't told me.'

'About what?'

'What do you think? I've been trying to get it out of you all night.'

Tom needs a long moment to realise what he was talking about. 'One thing for sure,' he finally says, 'I'm not going to die a fucking virgin.'

'A fucking virgin?' Kenny says, and Tom manages a small laugh.

'It's easing,' he says. 'Oh, fuck, thank Christ. It's easing.' He laughs again, more loudly, a mixture of relief and embarrassment. His tone is forced and hearty, covering its recent tracks. 'We'll try again. You do the jumping.'

'I think we should save our energy.'

'Then crack another joke. It was the joke that did the trick.'

Laughter on demand proves impossible; all the jokes Kenny has ever heard seem to have done a moonlight flit from his mind, untraceably. 'I could sing a song,' he says.

'What song?'

'Any song. Baa, baa black sheep. Twinkle, twinkle little star.'

Tom's voice is edgy with panic again: 'The other leg's cramping. Jesus – think of something. You're the brains of this outfit.'

For the first time Kenny wonders if he might be close to cramp himself. He shoves the thought from his mind. Old voodoo habits: to think a fear is to make it real, to conjure it up. Then suddenly he is too busy for such thoughts; Tom has rolled onto his belly, and is clawing at him again, pushing him under.

'We're going to drown. We're going to fucking drown.'

A stray finger pokes Kenny's eye; he instinctively twists free and kicks away a metre. 'Where are you? Oh, Jesus – you giving up on me?'

'Just letting go for a few seconds. I need to piss.'

'Piss here. You've got to hold me.'

Tom's plea is gurgled through a swallowed mouthful of water, but Kenny kicks further away into the darkness. A horror story from the paper some weeks before comes back to him: of a married couple who hit a reef somewhere out among the islands, and took to the water in life-jackets. The woman had been injured in the collision; after a few hours in the water, sharks began to nibble at her torn legs. Reef sharks, not quite big enough to end it quickly, but big enough to tear off small mouthfuls: toes, fingers, chunks of calf and thigh.

Knowing she could not survive, the woman had told her husband to swim away. And he had swum away, into the night, his wife lost to him, being eaten alive, her cries chasing him through the darkness. 'Help me, Jesus, Kenny – help me!'

Kenny silently eases his head beneath the surface of the water, croc-fashion, and kicks further away from his friend. He surfaces some distance off, but senses that Tom might still locate him.

'Help me! Help! ... Help me!' The gurgled cries carom between the high walls, amplified terribly. Even more terrible is the short silence that follows.

'I'll help if you don't fucking panic!' Kenny shouts. 'I'll help if you shut the fuck up!'

Tom breaks surface, swallowing water, choking as much as shouting. Hiding in the darkmost corner, the thought comes to Kenny that if he waits till the noise subsides, waits till Tom has nearly drowned, he might then resuscitate him, and hold him afloat, becalmed, in the Correct Life-Saving Position till dawn. He listens to his friend's frantic shouts and splashings, staying mum. He is acting only partly on instinct; he also knows exactly what he is doing. And knows that he knows, a realisation that fills him with anger. That anger is easily turned against Tom. Dumb, drunk Tom. Scared, panicky Tom – who would have thought it? The noise of his begging fills the chamber – 'Somebody – help me! Please!' Tears fill Kenny's already wet eyes. He slips his head beneath the surface to wash away the heat of those tears, but the flail of Tom's struggles is only amplified by the medium of water. Kenny even fancies he can hear the voice calling to him underwater, gasping a last burble of syllables, a bubbling Kenny, Kenny. Or is it – it might be – mummy, mummy? He surfaces, and this time swims towards these desperate, choking sounds, unable to keep his distance.

'Tom?' he shouts. 'Tommy?'

Tom has vanished.

'You stupid bastard,' he shouts. 'You stupid fucking bastard! Where are you? If you are fucking hiding from me!'

He duckdives beneath the surface repeatedly, groping in the dark water with hands that grasp nothing. His legs and arms soon ache; exhausted, he turns onto his back to rest, but floating also soon becomes an ordeal. The great mass of fresh water seems no longer able to support him, or else he cannnot relax. He chokes on a swallowed mouthful, but without panic; he is too weary for panic. He feels dulled, numbed, emptied even of anger.

His unfeeling mind is nevertheless capable of thought. The hour must be ... 3 a.m.? Four? An hour or two, at most, till daybreak, and someone spots the abandoned Mercedes. Will he have enough energy to shout? And if so, how often? Regularly, like the sweep of a lighthouse? Once every ten seconds? Once a minute? And what of cramp? The possibility has become unworrying, as if the capacity for fear has also drained from him, his reserves of adrenaline, the raw fuel of worry, consumed by the ordeals of the night. The problem of cramp seems no more than that: a problem to solve, a kind of algebra, remote from real events and things.

A large object bumps gently, surprisingly, against him as he floats, and rebounds slowly from the collision, an astronaut adrift in space.

'Tom?'

He reaches out a hand and grabs at an arm. Tom is floating face-up – what does that mean? He remembers that drowned women float face-up, but men, for some reason, face-down. Might Tom still be alive, then? Still breathing? His earlier plan, or self-justification, seems plausible again: wait till drowning has calmed Tom, then resuscitate him. He tugs the floating body towards him, treading water.

Lifesaving Certificate routines come back to him: he pinches the nostrils shut between the thumb and forefinger of his right hand; with his left he hooks down the chin to open the mouth. Leaning his elbow and shoulder on the half-submerged body he presses his open mouth onto Tom's, and breathes out, hard. The mouth is cold and wet, and carries the faint taste of sour, regurgitated sherry, but Kenny is beyond squeamishness. The downward pressure of his mouth pushes Tom's head beneath the surface, but he senses a slight inflation of the chest against his elbow. He senses this, also: as the chest inflates, the body rides higher in the water, made more buoyant.

When he removes his mouth the chest relaxes, the drowned man exhales, a dead man breathing, and the body re-submerges perceptibly. A strange thing: the body is cold to touch, water-temperature, but its breath is warmish, released from a still-warm interior.

He presses his mouth to the other mouth again, and again, but the effort of keeping his friend's head above water is exhausting. His heart pounds, his own breaths come in large gasps; he floats for a time, breathing slowly and deeply, trying to calm himself. Then realises he has released Tom without noticing; the body has drifted away into darkness – only a few feet away – and rolled face-down. He thinks again of how the body rode higher in the water when its lungs were buoyed by air. The body? Its? He almost winces, to find himself thinking this way – but shame also seems beyond his exhausted emotions. The words are surely necessary instruments of thinking, long-handled tongs, keeping emotion at a distance. His survival might depend on such tongs. His mind grasps again at the thought: inflating the lungs buoys the body. Might he use it as a life-buoy? He had refused to allow the drowning man to cling to him; might he now cling to the drowned? He rolls the body over like a log, and by pressing his weight onto the torso levers the face above water. He turns the head to one side, hooks open the mouth with two fingers and drains out as much water as possible. As before, he breathes into the mouth, pinching the nostrils, and is gratified as the lungs fill and expand. A small gush of water escapes as he takes his mouth away; he takes a quick deep breath and applies his mouth again. A sigh of air escapes after the second inflation. How many breaths can two water-logged lungs hold? He breathes again, and again, forcefully, holding the mouth closed between breaths, until a blurt of air escaping under pressure between the squeezed lips tells him he has reached end-point. Keeping the nostrils and mouth pinched shut with his right hand, he floats now without effort, half-supported by the inflated body, as if by an inner-tube or life-preserver. Absurd images from a childhood spent in swimming pools clog his head: car-tyres, rubber ducks, inflatable crocodiles, arm-floaties. Floatie. The child's word sounds grotesque; he feels a sudden urge to laugh, a desire to laugh, sensing also that by laughing he might be able to cry.

Neither proves possible.

After some minutes his clenched right hand begins to cramp. A better idea: clamping nose and mouth shut with his left hand he peels the jocks from the body with his right, flexing the knees, tugging them down, then finally pushing them from the feet with his own feet. After a top-up inflation, he stuffs the sodden garment into the mouth, wedging it with two fingers deeply inside the throat, blocking the escape of air from both nose and mouth.

Now he floats more comfortably, sprawled across the submerged torso, feet trailing. The coldness of the water strikes him for the first time since he has leapt from the high ledge, hours before. He shivers slightly, but only briefly, for the air on his exposed arms and head is humidly warm. The body beneath him, its face a few inches from his, begins to resume a human identity, begins to reclaim its proper name: Tom, his friend. He log-rolls it again, face-down, more to prevent the escape of air from the mouth, he tells himself, than to avoid the nearness of that face. He remembers, suddenly, the sherry flagon. Might it still be bobbing on the surface, close at hand? Could Tom have used it as a life-support? Why hadn't they thought of it? Too drunk? Too panicked? Of course it must have filled with water and sunk. Other, more random thoughts begin to jump in and out of his head, of the kind that visit exhausted brains, late at night: weird, disconnected patterns of recent events, of school, home, his parents' absence, Debbie and Tom on the beach, long ago now, years in the past. From this half-conscious delirium he might have drifted more deeply into sleep, but the noise of passing birds overhead – the screech of black parrots – rouses him. He lifts his head. The square screen of sky above is fading from black to pale blue, the wispy shreds of cloud are reddening with the usual tropic abruptness. The inside walls of the great tank have already emerged from darkness, and with them the rusting ladder, bolted to the northern side, its lowest rung a good body-length above the water level.

No rain has fallen in the night, although somewhere thunder is grumbling again, and lightning is planting its stiletto heel upon the earth: a faint tremor in the air, an invisible ripple in the water. It seems to Kenny that now, at last, the Wet is no more than a few hours away: an idle thought, another day's conversation starter. As he clings to the cold, buoyant body he speaks the words aloud, finding comfort in their familiar social surface, beneath which trembles only the faintest anxiety, a sensation which he can't fully identify, and is still too weary to bring into sharper focus, but which seems to settle at last on the memory of the dusty car outside, his father's precious Mercedes, unsheltered, windows wound down, soon to be rained on, and in.

NOTES ON THE CONTRIBUTORS

MATT CONDON Matt Condon is the author of several works of fiction. His latest novel is *The Pillow Fight*. He lives in Sydney. 'Incident in the Hotel Tangier' is an excerpt from *The Lime Bar Arias*, to be published by Penguin Books in 2001.

CHRIS DAFFEY Chris Daffey was born in Melbourne in 1972. He worked as a lawyer for a number of years before resigning to write his first book, forthcoming from Penguin Books in 2001. 'Tea and Biscuits with Richie Benaud' is an extract from that book. Email Chris on chrisdaffey@bigpond.com

FRANK DALBY DAVISON Frank Dalby Davison was the author of the short-story collections *The Woman at the Mill* and *The Road to Yesterday*, and novels including *Dusty*, *Man-Shy* and *The White Thorntree*.

MICHELLE DE KRETSER Michelle de Kretser was born in Sri Lanka. She now lives in Melbourne. 'Life with Sea Views' won the 1999 *Age* Short Story Competition. Michelle is also the author of the bestselling novel *The Rose Grower*.

NICK EARLS Nick Earls is the author of the bestselling novels *Zigzag Street*, *Bachelor Kisses* and *Perfect Skin*. He has also written two award-winning novels for young adults, *After January* and *48 Shades of Brown*, and the collection of stories *Headgames*. Nick Earls' work has been published internationally in English and in translation. His previous jobs include suburban GP and storytelling armchair. He lives in Brisbane.

HELEN GARNER Helen Garner has been publishing novels, short stories and non-fiction since 1977 when her first novel, *Monkey Grip*, appeared. Her most recent books are *True Stories*, a collection of 25 years of feature journalism, and *My Hard Heart*, her selected short fiction. She lives in Melbourne.

PETER GOLDSWORTHY Peter Goldsworthy's most recent book is a revised version of his novella, *Jesus Wants Me for a Sunbeam*. His *New and Selected Poems* is due to appear next May in Australia and the UK. 'The Kiss' was first published in the *Adelaide Review*.

NOTES ON THE CONTRIBUTORS

DEREK HANSEN Derek Hansen is the author of the bestselling novels *Lunch with the Generals*, *Lunch with Mussolini*, *Sole Survivor*, *Blockade* and, most recently, *Perfect Couple*. He has also written the short story collections *Dead Fishy* and *Psycho Cat*. Derek Hansen's work has been published in America, Great Britain, Europe and the Republic of China. He is married with two adult children and lives on Sydney's northern beaches.

SHIRLEY HAZZARD Shirley Hazzard is the author of a short-story collection, *The Cliffs of Fall*, and four novels, *The Evening of the Holiday*, *People in Glass Houses*, *The Bay of Noon* and *The Transit of Venus*.

ELIZABETH JOLLEY Elizabeth Jolley is acclaimed as one of Australia's leading writers and has received an Order of Australia, honorary doctorates from WAIT (now Curtin University) and Macquarie and Queensland universities, and the ASAL Gold Medal for her contribution to Australian literature, as well as many major Australian awards for her fiction. Her latest novel is *An Accommodating Spouse*.

MATTHEW KARPIN Matthew Karpin is the author of a novella, *In Our Own Day*. His stories have recently appeared in *Sislo*, *Imago*, *Heat* and the anthology *Enough Already*. 'What are the Roots that Clutch' is an extract from his first novel, a work in progress entitled *Argument from Silence*. Another extract from the novel will appear in *Meanjin* early in 2001.

NOTES ON THE CONTRIBUTORS

CHANDANI LOKUGÉ Chandani Lokugé is the author of the novel *If the Moon Smiled* and *Moth and Other Stories*. Her short stories have been widely anthologised, including in the *Penguin Anthology of Modern Sri Lankan Stories*. She is Editor for Oxford University Press of a series of Indian women's autobiographies and fiction. She is currently writing her second novel, to be published by Penguin Books.

DAVID MALOUF David Malouf is one of Australia's most admired authors. He has written poetry, essays, a play, novels and short stories. His novels include *Johnno*, *Fly Away Peter*, *An Imaginary Life* and *Remembering Babylon*, which was shortlisted for the Booker Prize. He has won awards including the IMPAC Dublin Literary Award, the New South Wales Premier's Literary Award, the *Age* Book of the Year Award, the Miles Franklin Award and the Commonwealth Prize for Fiction.

MONICA MCINERNEY Monica McInerney grew up in Clare, South Australia, in a family of seven children. She has lived in Adelaide, London, Sydney, Melbourne, Dublin and Hobart and worked in publishing, public relations, marketing, children's television and music pubs. She is working on her second novel, also set in Ireland and Australia. 'A Taste for It' is an excerpt from her forthcoming novel of the same name, to be published by Penguin Books in 2001.

NOTES ON THE CONTRIBUTORS

GILLIAN MEARS Gillian Mears lives and writes in Nymboida NSW. She is the author of *Ride a Cock Horse*, *Fineflour* and *The Mint Lawn*. She is presently completing a novel and short story collection.

JULIE SIMPSON Julie Simpson is the daughter of the late great Australian travel writer Colin Simpson. She spent many years as a program maker with the ABC, and wrote and illustrated eight children's books for Studio Vista in London in the early seventies. Her latest book is *Idle Hour in the County of Hope*.

ELIZABETH STEAD Elizabeth Stead was born in Sydney in 1932, and has had numerous short stories published. Her first novel, *The Fishcastle*, was published by Penguin Books in 2000.

AMY WITTING Amy Witting was born in Annandale, New South Wales, in 1918. She has published five novels, three collections of short stories, two books of verse and a book of poetry. Amy Witting has had numerous poems and short stories published in magazines such as *Quadrant* and *The New Yorker*. In 1993 she was awarded the Patrick White Prize and in 2000 she won the *Age* Book of the Year Award for her novel *Isobel on the Way to the Corner Shop*.

ACKNOWLEDGEMENTS

Grateful acknowledgement is due to the following authors and publishers for permission to reprint stories in this collection.

MATT CONDON 'Incident in the Hotel Tangier' was first published in a slightly different form in the *Adelaide Review* in 1999. It is an excerpt from *The Lime Bar Arias*, to be published by Penguin Books in 2001. Reproduced by permission of Penguin Books Australia Ltd and the author.

CHRIS DAFFEY 'Tea and Biscuits with Richie Benaud' is an extract from the forthcoming novel *Impressing Jenny*, to be published by Penguin Books. Reproduced by permission of Penguin Books Australia Ltd and the author.

FRANK DALBY DAVISON 'The Wasteland', taken from *The Wells of Beersheba and Other Stories*, © Estate of Frank Dalby Davison 1970, 1985, is reproduced by permission of HarperCollins*Publishers*.

MICHELLE DE KRETSER 'Life with Sea Views' was first published in the *Age*. Reprinted in this collection by permission of Michelle de Kretser.

NICK EARLS 'The Haircut of a More Successful Man', from *Headgames*, published by Penguin Books, 1999. Reprinted in this collection by courtesy of Curtis Brown (Australia) Pty Ltd and the author.

HELEN GARNER 'All Those Bloody Young Catholics', from *My Hard Heart*, published by Penguin Books Australia Ltd, 1998 (first collected in *Postcards from Surfers*, McPhee Gribble Publishers, 1985). Reproduced by permission of Penguin Books Australia Ltd and the author.

PETER GOLDSWORTHY 'The Kiss' was first published in the *Adelaide Review* as 'The Water Tank'. Reproduced by permission of the author.

DEREK HANSEN 'The Absolute Authority on Everything', from *Dead Fishy*, Mandarin Books, 1995. Reproduced by permission of Margaret Connolly Associates and the author.

SHIRLEY HAZZARD 'Villa Adriana' was first published in the short story collection *Cliffs of Fall* (Knopf, 1963).

ACKNOWLEDGEMENTS

ELIZABETH JOLLEY 'Dingle the Fool', from *Fellow Passengers*, published by Penguin Books Australia Ltd 1997, was first published in *Quadrant* in 1972. Reproduced by permission of Penguin Books Australian Ltd and the author.

MATTHEW KARPIN 'What are the Roots that Clutch', first published in *Heat* 14, is reproduced by permission of the author.

CHANDANI LOKUGÉ 'Pipe Dream' was first published in *Optimus: Special 50th Anniversary Issue No. 1: Celebrating Women*, No. 13, 1st Quarter, 1998. Reproduced by permission of the author.

DAVID MALOUF Copyright © David Malouf 2000. Reproduced by permission of the author c/o Rogers, Coleridge & White Ltd., 20 Powis Mews, London W11 1JN.

MONICA McINERNEY 'A Taste for It' is an excerpt from Monica McInerney's forthcoming novel of the same name. Reproduced by permission of Penguin Books Australia Ltd and the author.

GILLIAN MEARS 'Eileen's Christmas Fudge' is reproduced by permission of Curtis Brown Australia Pty Ltd and the author.

ACKNOWLEDGEMENTS

JULIE SIMPSON 'Mermaid Beach', from *Idle Hour in the County of Hope*, is reprinted with permission of Hodder Headline 2000.

ELIZABETH STEAD 'Five Unusual Journeys' is reproduced with kind permission of *Southerly* magazine, University of Sydney, and the author.

AMY WITTING 'Theatre Comes to Wombat Creek', from *Faces and Voices*, published by Penguin Books Australia Ltd 2000, first appeared in the *Bulletin*. Reproduced by permission of Penguin Books Australia Ltd and the author.